THE DALAI LAMA

MODERN SPIRITUAL MASTERS
Robert Ellsberg, Series Editor

Already published:

MODERN SPIRITUAL MASTERS SERIES

THE DALAI LAMA

Essential Writings

Selected with an Introduction by

THOMAS A. FORSTHOEFEL

ORBIS BOOKS

Maryknoll, New York 10545

Founded in 1970, Orbis Books endeavors to publish works that enlighten the mind, nourish the spirit, and challenge the conscience. The publishing arm of the Maryknoll Fathers and Brothers, Orbis seeks to explore the global dimensions of the Christian faith and mission, to invite dialogue with diverse cultures and religious traditions, and to serve the cause of reconciliation and peace. The books published reflect the views of their authors and do not represent the official position of the Maryknoll Society. To learn more about Maryknoll and Orbis Books, please visit our website at www.maryknoll.org.

Library of Congress Cataloging-in-Publication Data

Bstan-'dzin-rgya-mtsho, Dalai Lama XIV, 1935–
    [Selections. English. 2008]
    The Dalai Lama : essential writings / edited with an introduction by
Thomas A. Forsthoefel.
        p. cm. – (Modern spiritual masters series)
    ISBN-13: 978-1-57075-789-1
    1. Religious life – Buddhism. I. Forsthoefel, Thomas A. II. Title.
BQ7935.B772 2008
294.3'923 – dc22
                                                    2008015967

Contents

Acknowledgments

I gratefully acknowledge the following publishers who have granted permission to draw from the following sources:

The Art of Happiness: A Handbook for the Living, by Dalai Lama and Howard C. Cutler, copyright © 1998 by H.H. Dalai Lama and Howard C. Cutler. Used by permission of Riverhead Books, an imprint of Penguin Group (USA) Inc.

Ethics for the New Millennium, by Dalai Lama and Alexander Norman, copyright © 1999 by His Holiness The Dalai Lama. Used by permission of Riverhead Books, an imprint of Penguin Group (USA) Inc. Copyright © 1997 by His Holiness the Dalai Lama, reprinted with permission of The Wylie Agency, Inc.

The Universe in a Single Atom: The Convergence of Science and Spirituality, by His Holiness The Dalai Lama, copyright © 2005 The Dalai Lama. Used by permission of an imprint of The Doubleday Broadway Publishing, a division of Random House, Inc.

Violence and Compassion: Conversations with the Dalai Lama, trans. by Jean Claude-Carriere, translation copyright © 1996 by Doubleday, a division of Bantam Doubleday Dell Publishing group. Used by permission of Doubleday, a division of Random House, Inc.

An Open Heart, by His Holiness The Dalai Lama, copyright © 2001 by His Holiness the Dalai Lama. Used by permission of Little, Brown & Company.

Healing Anger: The Power of Patience from a Buddhist Perspective, by The Dalai Lama, trans. Geshe Thupten Jinpa, copyright © 1997 His Holiness the Dalai Lama, whose sole agent for these teachings is Arizona Teachings, Inc. Used by permission of Snow Lion Publications, www.snowlionpub.com.

A Policy of Kindness: An Anthology of Writings by and about the Dalai Lama, foreword by Senator Claiborne Pell, compiled and edited by Sidney Piburn, copyright © 1990 Sidney Piburn. Used by permission of Snow Lion Publications, www.snowlionpub.com.

The Path to Enlightenment, by H.H. the Dalai Lama, ed. and trans. by Glenn H. Mullin, copyright © 1982 His Holiness Tenzin Gyatso Dalai Lama XIV, copyright © 1995 H.H. the Dalai Lama and Glenn H. Mullin. Used by permission of Snow Lion Publications, www.snowlionpub.com.

Stages of Meditation, by the Dalai Lama, root text by Kamalashila, trans. by Venerable Geshe Lobsang Jordhen, Losang Choepel Canchenpa, and Jeremy Russell, copyright © 2001 His Holiness the Dalai Lama. Used by permission of Snow Lion Publications, www.snowlionpub.com.

Path of Wisdom, Path of Peace: A Personal Conversation, by His Holiness the Dalai Lama and Felizitas von Schonborn, foreword by Wei Jingsheng, trans. by Christine M. Grimm, copyright © 2004 by Diogenes Verlag AG, Zurich; English translation copyright © 2005 by The Crossroad Publishing Company. Used by permission of The Crossroad Publishing Company via the Copyright Clearance Center.

Advice on Dying and Living a Better Life, by His Holiness the Dalai Lama, trans. and ed. by Jeffrey Hopkins, Ph.D., copyright © 2002 by His Holiness the Dalai Lama and Jeffrey Hopkins,

Sources

Advice on Dying and Living a Better Life. Trans. and ed. Jeffrey Hopkins. New York: Atria Books, 2002.

The Art of Happiness: A Handbook for Living, with Howard C. Cutler, M.D. New York: Riverhead Books, 1998.

The Buddhism of Tibet. Trans. and ed. Jeffrey Hopkins. Ithaca, N.Y.: Snow Lion Publications, 1975.

Essence of the Heart Sutra: The Dalai Lama's Heart of Wisdom Teachings. Trans. and ed. Geshe Thupten Jinpa. Boston: Wisdom Publications, 2005.

Ethics for the New Millennium. New York: Riverhead Books, 1999. Copyright © 1997 by His Holiness the Dalai Lama, reprinted with permission of The Wylie Agency, Inc.

The Four Noble Truths. Trans. Geshe Thupten Jinpa, ed. Dominique Side. London: Thorsons, 1997.

Freedom in Exile: The Autobiography of the Dalai Lama. New York: Harper Collins, 1990.

The Good Heart: A Buddhist Perspective on the Teachings of Jesus. Intro. Laurence Freeman, trans. Geshe Thupten Jinpa, ed. Robert Kiely. Boston: Wisdom Publications, 1998.

Healing Anger: The Power of Patience from a Buddhist Perspective. Trans. Geshe Thupten Jinpa. Ithaca, N.Y.: Snow Lion Publications, 1997.

The Heart of Compassion: A Practical Approach to a Meaningful Life. Twin Lakes, Wisc.: Lotus Press, 1997.

How to Expand Love: Widening the Circle of Loving Relationships. Trans. and ed. Jeffrey Hopkins. New York: Atria Books, 2005.

How to Practice the Way to a Meaningful Life. Trans. and ed. Jeffrey Hopkins. New York: Atria Books, 2002.

How to See Yourself as You Really Are. Trans. and ed. Jeffrey Hopkins. New York: Atria Books, 2006.

The Meaning of Life from a Buddhist Perspective. Trans. and ed. Jeffrey Hopkins. Boston: Wisdom Publications, 1992.

MindScience: An East-West Dialogue, with Herbert Benson, Robert A. F. Thurman, Howard E. Gardner, Daniel Goleman, and participants in the Harvard Mind Science Symposium. Ed. Daniel Goleman and Robert A. F. Thurman. Boston: Wisdom Publications, 1991.

An Open Heart: Practicing Compassion in Everyday Life. Ed. Nicholas Vreeland. Boston: Little, Brown, 2001.

Path of Wisdom, Path of Peace: A Personal Conversation, with Felizitas Von Schonborn. Trans. Christine M. Grimm. New York: Crossroad, 2002.

The Path to Enlightenment. Ed. and trans. Glenn Mullin. Ithaca, N.Y.: Snow Lion Publications, 1982.

A Policy of Kindness. Compiled and ed. Sidney Piburn. Ithaca, N.Y.: Snow Lion Publications, 1990.

The Power of Compassion. Trans. Geshe Thupten Jinpa. New Delhi: Indus, 1995.

Stages of Meditation. Trans. Venerable Geshe Lobsang Jordhen, Losang Choepel Ganchenpa, and Jeremy Russell. Ithaca, N.Y.: Snow Lion, 2001.

The Universe in a Single Atom: The Convergence of Science and Spirituality. New York: Morgan Road Books, 2005.

Violence and Compassion: Dialogues on Life Today, with Jean-Claude Carriere. New York: Doubleday, 1994.

Introduction

The Teachings of Buddhism

Encounter

Some years ago I had the privilege of meeting the Dalai Lama.
I should qualify that. I can't exactly say I "met" him, because
I did not enjoy any formal introductions. I was one of over a
hundred participants at a conference in Dharamsala, his home
and the site of the Tibetan government in exile. He listened
with keen attentiveness to the proceedings of the conference and
occasionally offered questions and observations. I had been in
India several times before as part of the research and training
required for a Ph.D. in Indian religion and philosophy. And
I had already taught Buddhism for a number of years, so I
was well acquainted with the central elements of Buddhist history and philosophy. But being in Dharamsala and witnessing
the calm serenity of the Tibetan monks seemed to generate a
new depth of understanding of Buddhism naturally and without
argument.

This movement of heart and mind was deepened when I
did, in fact, "meet" the Dalai Lama. At the end of the conference, in a small hall with walls covered by tanghkas, the
Dalai Lama received each participant personally. When it was
my turn to greet him, the Dalai Lama took both my hands and
gazed at me. It took a moment for me to gain my bearings;
for a moment my mind was scattered, marked by anxiety and
self-consciousness. After a moment of such mental "dispersal,"

I quickly collected myself and became very aware that the Dalai Lama, in my view, was doing something that far transcended typical mundane encounters. This was no back-slapping, "How 'bout them Bulls!" Instead, the encounter was something deeper and more penetrating, which I later flippantly characterized as being zapped by the Dalai Lama's mojo. The Indian religious traditions greatly revere the act of beholding the divine in its many manifestations. According to this view, something very special and transformative occurs through the sacred exchange of sight. In India, this is called *darshan*, "seeing," and implies both seeing and being seen by the divine. In such encounters, a power (*shakti*) is transmitted, perhaps conferring some grace or enhancing some capacity in the beholder. This "exchange" can occur in temples, at holy sites in nature, and in the presence of a holy one.

In a recent book, *Soulsong*, I tried to account for the ways in which we are "zapped" by others, the holy ones in our lives. And a central premise of the book is this: the holy ones in our lives become mirrors of our own becoming. In some sense, we see ourselves. This does not mean we are to follow lockstep the patterns of another's path. But it means we perceive cardinal values and virtues in the life and example of another, and these strike deep chords within us; they resonate, and such resonance can only mean that those values and virtues are ours, too; otherwise, they would not ring so clearly in us. Something quickens, some primal moment of recognition, an "aha" moment in the deepest sense of the word: *I* want to be like that. *I* want that. And perhaps, most important of all, "*I* am that too," because those virtues already present in us resonate in the presence of the other; in such an encounter we feel the invitation to become more who we already are. The holy ones of our lives — and this cohort is hardly limited to Nobel Peace Prize winners but includes every person in our lives who shows us something of how to be here, how to be more human and therefore more divine — become mirrors of our own becoming.

This notion seemed to be conveyed in the Martin Scorcese film *Kundun* ("The Presence," an epithet for the Dalai Lama). The film represents the life and training of the young Dalai Lama and his eventual escape from the Chinese in 1950. When the young Dalai Lama crosses safely into India, he is asked his identity by the Indian border guards. The Dalai Lama responds, "I think I am a reflection, like the moon on water. When you see me, and I try to be a good man, you see yourself."

So when I say I "met" the Dalai Lama, I met myself in some fundamental way. This is not to imply superpowers or extraordinary heroism. I am as flawed and limited as anyone else. But something resonated, and though I had long been committed to spiritual values and teachings, a new or renewed awareness or resolve was quickened, too. I returned to the United States, but hardly with any magical transformation, some instant new-and-improved "Tom." Most of us at least remotely familiar with the organic process of psychological and spiritual development recognize that radical "soul makeovers" are few and far between. In fact, a radical soul makeover usually is neither possible nor desirable; we are who we are after all, and perhaps the most important element of the spiritual path may be finally coming to terms with ourselves, that is, finally accepting who we are in all our gifts and incongruities. "Mountaintop" experiences provide a welcome respite from the flurry of our busy-ness, and they can be useful: they crystallize again and again our clearest priorities. But transformation, in the end, isn't becoming something you are *not;* it is becoming more who you are. And this seems to happen more soundly when slow and sure, as yeast inevitably, inexorably leavens the bread.

The Contemporary Appeal of Buddhism in the West

The example and teaching of the Dalai Lama might be considered a leavening element too. For many years now, he has been indefatigable in teaching the central precepts of Buddhist philosophy to a world that seems particularly hungry for it. He travels the world, an ambassador of kindness with a popularity typically reserved for rock stars. He gives public addresses to audiences in the thousands, writes or co-writes endless best-sellers, attends or convenes conferences drawing the brightest thinkers in science and religion, confers with political leaders from around the globe. Why such popularity and impact at this time? I would suggest two reasons, one sociological, another anthropological.

One the one hand, the rise of the popularity of the Dalai Lama can be read in concert with the rise of the popularity of Buddhism in the West. We might suggest that Western culture has encountered a kind of impoverishment obtaining from the tensions of modernity and postmodernity. The crush of two world wars belied the drive and optimism of modernity and "human progress," and the oppressive force of cold war dualisms, crass capitalism, and increasing cynicism seemed to cascade in the "postmodern" world. In the postmodern world, faith in absolutes was eroded by reason, empirical evidence, and science. In addition to this, the church, in its various institutional operations, seemed to widen alienation by patterns of control, sexism, and patriarchy. For many in the West — disaffected Christians and Jews, agnostics, and even atheists — the time was ripe to hear something new. This "something new" may not really be new at all, at least in terms of ethics and virtue, but the framework, structure, and method of the teaching was indeed new for many in the West.

Buddhism, if anything, is eminently rational, psychological, and therapeutic. It squarely invests the burden of spiritual growth and progress onto the "hearer." In this, we see a high demand for personal accountability and responsibility matched with a concomitant resistance to any external authority or power to determine one's spiritual trajectory. Such starting points, I would suggest, may be particularly compelling to those unmoored or estranged by traditional religious or cultural forms. For persons alienated by concepts of God that import or repeat cultural patterns of sexism and patriarchy, a religion that has very little to do with this "God" may seem particularly attractive. And yet, while it may be true that Buddhism is not about "belief in God," we should be very careful neither to reduce Buddhism to philosophical materialism nor to impose un-nuanced or simplistic notions of God onto other traditions. If "God" is understood as a deified male sitting on a throne, then, yes, Buddhism certainly rejects this notion. But so do most mature Christians. If by "God" we might understand something far more profound, unnamable in any final way, some state both transcendent and immanent, then there is a rich space for dialogue about the nature and content of this state between Christian theologians and Buddhist philosophers.

This segues to the second element, the anthropological. In my view, a key feature of our anthropology is a holy longing, a longing for contact with the divine, however that divine is construed across cultures. The unfathomably rich diversity of religious and poetic expression across time and space bears witness to this human longing. I would say it is far too simplistic to hold that the vast mass of humanity from its earliest beginnings has been wholly beholden to "wish fulfillment" or other benighted psychological (Freud) or economic (Marx) patterns. The evidence to the contrary is there. And it cuts across cultures and shows itself in a rich array of patterns and symbols and ritual practices. If there is an anthropological impulse or need, and if traditional postmodern social and religious patterns have revealed their poverties, this need will find expression elsewhere. It is a need that will be met and must be met, for it expresses an essential dimension of human being. This dimension was called *homo religiosus* by the historian of religion Mircea Eliade. The orientation to the sacred characterizes our humanity more fundamentally than, say, the "mere" rational element denoted by *homo sapiens*. In a way, the human longing for the sacred is similar to the human need for intimacy. In fact, intimacy with the sacred is on the same continuum as intimacy itself. Relationship becomes a sacred site; in its best moments, "God" becomes embodied in human love. And since intimacy is a basic human need, people typically seek to meet that need when feeling its poignant absence. Similarly, in a world in which a gaping abyss reveals the emptiness of social and religious forms, new expressions emerge to meet the human need for sacred intimacy or transcendent connection. While some newer expressions sometimes appear to be unusual or even disconcerting, others have stood the test of time. These include the religions and philosophies of the East, perhaps especially Buddhism.

The Life of the Dalai Lama

Before I address the teachings of the Dalai Lama, let me say a word about his life. I will not repeat what has been recounted elsewhere in formal biographies or documentaries, but will, for the sake of context, highlight key elements of his biography. First, the Dalai Lama of course is Tibetan, and this cultural fact has decisively shaped his spiritual and intellectual formation. Second, the Dalai Lama was raised in Tibet during a time of bitter, intense, and deadly geopolitical conflict with China.

These two facts, taken together, set the stage for the singular unfolding of an extraordinary human being.

The Dalai Lama was born on July 6, 1935, in the village of Takster in the northeast Tibetan province of Amdo, near China. The young Dalai Lama, born Lhamo Thondup, was one of sixteen children born to his mother, seven of whom survived to adulthood. Two of his brothers were already Buddhist monks when Thondup was born, and the eldest, Thupten Jigme Norbu, was already recognized as a reincarnation of a spiritual master, called a *lama* or *tulku*. So the simplicity and humility of a large, extended, farming family set in the backdrop of Buddhist culture became the staging ground for a momentous development in Thondup's personal history and indeed, the contemporary history of Tibet.

Tibetan Buddhism affirms the doctrine of reincarnation, holding that our actions in this lifetime shape or condition our consciousness. The outcome of this causal process affects us in the current lifetime, in and through our habituated patterns and their typical consequences, but it extends into the next lifetime as well. Versions of this doctrine cut across most South Asian traditions, including Hinduism and Jainism. In the history of Tibetan Buddhism, the theory of reincarnated lamas emerged above all from the conviction in the compelling compassion found in great spiritual heroes who choose to be reincarnated for the good of sentient beings. However, a practical purpose contributed to it, too: the reincarnation of a particular lama established the spiritual lineage or authority of a tradition or monastery and, in case of the Dalai Lamas, established temporal authority over Tibet itself. Concerning the latter, the current Dalai Lama is the fourteenth in a line that extends back to the fourteenth century.

When the thirteenth Dalai Lama died in 1933, a process to determine his successor was instituted. This process included consulting oracles, discerning auspicious signs, and finally searching the provinces according to information gathered in the discernment process. When a party of monks, disguised as servants, came upon the family home of Thondup, the child recognized the senior monk as a lama from the great Sera monastery near Lhasa. Intrigued, the monks departed and returned days later bringing a number of artifacts belonging to the thirteenth Dalai Lama along with matching artifacts that did not. Thondup correctly pointed out each artifact properly belonging to the earlier Dalai Lama, saying, "It's mine. It's mine."[1] This and other developments indicated to the monks that the fourteenth Dalai Lama had been correctly identified.

The child was brought to Lhasa where, eventually, he began his extensive curriculum. Over time, this included not only the intense conceptual content of Buddhist philosophy, but also Tibetan art and culture, logic, Sanskrit, medicine, poetry, music and drama, and astrology. In addition, he was also introduced, even at a young age, to the structure and dynamics of Tibetan politics, being groomed for the day when he would ascend to power.

In 1950, the importance of his political training became clear: the Chinese invaded, claiming to liberate Tibet from "imperialist aggressors." In fact, though endowed with an unforgiving climate and difficult geography, Tibet, situated at the cusp of South Asia, was strategically important in China's geopolitical ambitions. As the Chinese gradually used military means to assert control over Tibet, increasing pressure on the Tibetan government forced a difficult and anguishing decision. In March 1959, after a failed uprising in Lhasa, the Dalai Lama fled to India, where, in the north Indian town of Dharamsala, the Tibetan government in exile was established. It is from here

---

1. The Dalai Lama, *Freedom in Exile* (New York: Harper Collins, 1990), 12.

that the Dalai Lama himself and the plight of Tibetan people gradually became known to the world. In the decades that followed the initial invasion and later repression, over one million Tibetans were killed by the Chinese and over six thousand monasteries were destroyed. Nevertheless, the Dalai Lama has effectively used the global stage to promote tirelessly the principles of wisdom and compassion, the cardinal virtues of all versions of Buddhism, as well as the call to justice, peace, and nonviolence, all of which issue from the teachings of Buddhism as well. For his extraordinary and resolute commitment to these principles, the Dalai Lama was awarded the Nobel Prize for Peace in 1989.

The Teachings of the Dalai Lama

The teachings of the Dalai Lama are the teachings of Buddhism proper. The Dalai Lama is a member of the Gelug pa order of Tibetan Buddhism, a tradition known for rigorous scholarship. Scholarship in Buddhism — I would venture in all scholastic traditions — is never mere intellectualism; it is rather critical study directed toward an end: greater intimacy with the sacred. We recall the tradition of "faith seeking understanding" in St. Anselm, the merging of Sufi mysticism and theology in the great Muslim thinker al-Ghazzali, and the great Talmudic debates of the Jewish rabbis. In Buddhism, similarly, the ultimate "end" of analytical inquiry is to see things as they are, freed of the distortions imposed by either intellect or emotion. Knowledge here, as in other traditions, is never just abstract "book knowledge" but instead is critical investigation of reality that issues in very real, practical outcomes: freedom from anguish and suffering. We might speak then of the soteriological impact of knowledge in Buddhism insofar as soteriology, in the world's religions, always investigates the questions and mechanisms of salvation.

I have grouped the writings of the Dalai Lama around three classic categories in Buddhist thought: wisdom, morality, and meditation. These three categories weave together; they come as a package, as it were, and they represent the three general categories that are found in the Eightfold Path, the practice of which leads to a deeper integration of Buddhist virtues. Such integration leads to increasing mental and ethical purity whose first fruit is a life of peace. While such peace may not itself be nirvana, it is, minimally, an important precondition for and first fruit of nirvana, for nirvana means the end of psychological states governed by greed and craving, anger and hostility, and the various distortions we impose upon phenomena owing to those impulses. Nirvana spells the decisive end of unwholesome mental states that cloud judgment. But to begin reigning in our recalcitrant mind, we also need to make incremental steps in purifying it, and this means practicing ethical behavior and cultivating virtue. This minimizes unwholesome obsessions and generates peace. Then, with a calmer mind, meditation becomes more natural, and our capacity for awareness expands. This issues, ultimately, in a breakdown of congenital egotism, a dissolution of a limited sense of self. And in the dissolution of self, according to Buddhism, one discovers the end of suffering.

Wisdom

For those in the West, Buddhist wisdom might mean many things, perhaps above all the stock content of Buddhist philosophy — the four Noble Truths, the theory of dependent origination, the five aggregates, emptiness doctrine, and so on. For Buddhists, wisdom simply(!) means "seeing things as they are," and that means seeing things free from the distortions imposed by the lens of self-centeredness. When we view things through the "eyeglass" of self, phenomena become charged by the polar impulses of attraction ("I've gotta have it") or aversion ("I've gotta get rid of it"). In this case, phenomena become magically transformed by our projections. If our mind is gripped by a "gotta have it" mentality, the reputed favorable qualities of an object are inflated and any negative ones are downplayed or ignored. On the other hand, if we find ourselves in a "gotta ged rid of it" mental state, the negative qualities of the object are exaggerated and the positive ones are dismissed or downplayed. Both cases reflect distortions based on self-centered desires. Nothing of course really happens to the object itself; the object is what it is. But in the end it becomes the locus of our projections. We are the ones whose mental state fluctuates according to the impulses of attraction or aversion. The object remains unchanged. This happens most soberly in relationships, when couples who adored and idealized each other "suddenly" see their partner's "egregious" flaws. And, though celibate, even the Dalai Lama recognizes the wild transformation, admitting that in some cases, "It may even be worth divorcing!"

In the grip of attraction-aversion, we sometimes marshal strategies to insure we get what we want or avoid what we don't want. But, for Buddhists, this is a recipe for suffering. We cannot control reality to fit our personal agenda or life trajectory in any absolute way. The unpredictability and instability of life trump our attempts to establish absolute or final notions of satisfaction based on self-centered desires. I recall the wry observation of the great scholar of Tibetan Buddhism Robert Thurman: "It's you against the universe, and we know whose going to lose that one." The truth is that things change, wear out, fade, die, transform. The truth is that weird things happen. Traumas, crises, conflicts, change. This is the nature of things. So to attempt to dodge this process or control it in some fundamental way for ongoing advantage will inevitably cause frustration and distress, because, in the end, we cannot control reality. Reality doesn't stay put. Things change. We suffer loss.

This is not intended to be a recipe for gloom, much less for a robot-like affect, but rather to equip us with a certain awareness so that our expectations are realistic. We all know how a Pollyanna-like optimism just doesn't sit right with us. It seems ungrounded, unreal. We also know how intense pessimism also just doesn't seem quite right. Both approaches in the end are unhelpful and perhaps even dangerous, owing to their severe incompleteness. Imagine if a doctor were overly optimistic or cheery about very grave symptoms or, on the other hand, were overly pessimistic about rather mild symptomology. In both cases, treatment plans might be woefully inappropriate and inadequate according to the circumstances. The best approach is a realistic approach, and Buddhism, if anything, is eminently realistic. And with such realism one is able to move through life a bit more smoothly, with greater ease, perhaps no longer overly ruffled by the vicissitudes of life, because life in the end is constituted by vicissitude. Change and flow are the nature of things. While the ultimate state of realization, nirvana, implies the decisive termination of unwholesome mental states, another take is that of the Japanese master Dogen Zenji, who held that impermanence *itself* is nirvana, a notion that could spin our usual concepts of loss and change on their heads. We often resist the reality of impermanence in our lives. This resistance is the source of our suffering. If we took a different approach — seeing change as the very nature of reality — our suffering would cease.

Buddhism speaks about Siddhartha's teachings as the turning of the wheel of dharma. For Buddhists, the teaching or dharma of the Buddha is true, and the internalization of it in our lives reduces friction, lubricates relationships, creates ease of movement. Curiously, automobile mechanics, when repairing wheels or brakes, sometimes comment, "The wheel is true." It moves smoothly, is balanced properly, free of frictions or impediments, and all this insures safety and freedom of movement. An amusing example of wheels that are *not* "true" and that therefore resist fluid movement are those unpleasant grocery carts that pull to one side. One seems required to wrestle with the cart merely to move it down the aisle. The outcome for the shopper: frustration. And frustration is a typical translation of *duhkha,* suffering, the first of the Buddha's Noble Truths. To say life is suffering means that in the absence of awareness, the axis of our lives will be skewed, out of balance, and therefore our emotional mobility will be limited. This will be frustrating. When life is "out of synch" with reality — when our lives are estranged from reality — we suffer.

Buddhism prepares us to see the truth of change in life. A corollary to the central truth of change is that nothing external to us can bring us lasting satisfaction. External events, like all other phenomena, are by definition transitory. But the psychological state that keys in on the object of satisfaction is the issue. This is desire, and particularly intense desire, craving, the cause of suffering. This is the second Noble Truth. Intense desire or craving tends to be unstable and escalating; it never seems to be tamped down, but rises up and reasserts itself, like the squawking baby robin with the open mouth: *feed me.* Desire is like the carpet that is just a tad oversized for the room. Push it down in one place, it pops up in another. Moreover, desire comes with a cost — frustration, longing, anxiety. Anger, too, may arise, particularly when the desire is unmet or blocked. Indeed, the intensity of desires can provoke serious conflict — in relationships, at work, in politics. And even if desires are fulfilled, they pass, and a repeated cycle of longing and frustration follows. Gotta have it (again). More and better. And more frequently than not. In the end, intense desire, craving, can never hold on to the thing it craves. It always slips through the fingers. It ends. The Buddhist answer to the roller coaster ride of desire is to get off the roller coaster. Terminate the cycle. Exercising restraint and discipline — choosing not to step on the roller coaster of self-centered concern — is the prescription for sanity. The awareness that terminating the cycle of self-centered desires brings peace is the third Noble Truth, and the method of doing that, following the spiritual path, is the fourth Noble Truth of the Buddha.

The Teaching of No-Soul

"Sanity" begins to recalibrate our "seeing," both internally and externally, above all by eliminating a hyper self-consciousness that issues in atomized selves in the universe each in competition and contention with the other. In the end, Buddhism dissolves the notion of self and, thereby, the selfishness that follows such notions. Here's how: Buddhist introspection reveals that impermanence, inescapably evident and often deeply poignant in the external world, applies to our internal world, too. What one discovers as one "goes within" is a constantly changing process of consciousness, itself acting in dynamic interrelationship with our feelings, ideas, and tendencies, not to mention our body or physical state. These five "aggregates" exhaustively account for what we mean by a "person" in Buddhism. But none of these aggregates are permanent enduring "things" or essences. For Buddhists, consciousness is not a permanent substrate of personality, our "real" me or soul. Buddhists do not hold what philosophers call a "substance theory" of identity, one in which the natural process of change affects "accidental" or secondary characteristics (say, the color of our hair) but does not change the "essence" or "nature" or "soul" of a person. Indeed, the word "substance" itself is illustrative. While it connotes something weighty or enduring (e.g., "substantive"), its etymology is indicative: "sub-stand," "standing under." For many thinkers (in the East, by the way, as well as in the West) "substance," "soul," and "nature," all suggest an unchanging substrate, the "real" me or you or essence of a thing, that which makes something x and not y. In this view, it's as if every item in the universe, let alone the grocery store, has a UPC code, which, when scanned, reveals it for what it was: *Ah, Book! Ah, Chair! Ah, You! Ah, Me!* This view, one that affirms the "nature" or "essence" or "soul" of a thing, has a long history in the West going back to Aristotle. It also has a long and powerful intellectual tradition in various schools of Hinduism in India.

But Buddhists reject essence- or substance-based theories of identity. If every phenomenal event "out there" is visibly and empirically changing, a complex mix of interacting, fluid phenomena, so is everything "in here." Penetrating analysis confirms what the monk Nagasena said at the end of a very famous dialogue with the inquisitive King Milinda: "There is no person here." By that he means, there is no isolatable, independent, permanent enduring essence here, but instead a streaming flow of changing phenomena, including body, sensations, ideas, volitional tendencies, and consciousness. Identity, in this view, is not picked out by "essence" but by causal connectedness. I certainly am not the same "Tom" as I was upon birth. I'm no longer eight pounds five ounces and I have a range of cognitive and emotional capacities that exceed those of an infant. Nor am I the same person as I

was in 1968, when I celebrated, as a ten-year-old, my beloved
Tigers, who won the World Series that year. Nor am I the same
person who was in the Jesuits for four years many years ago. Obviously, I am no longer these particular "incarnations," but I am
causally connected to them. I am intimately related to this particular "stream of events" perhaps a bit more proximately than, say,
the tree outside my window. For Buddhism, all things and persons
are constantly changing processes. Every person and object is a
stream of events, not concretized by a fixed "glue" of identity. For
Buddhists, far from being terrifying, this "absence of soul" is extremely good news, because it means we can grow, change, and develop. We do not need to be boxed in or box ourselves in with fixed
notions of who we are, which then require endless defense and
protection. We don't need to marshal strategies to reinforce our
sense of self for either our sake or the sake of others. We are free.

Consciousness, then, for Buddhists, is not a permanent soul
that ups and leaves the body upon death, but instead is a process that changes through dynamic interaction with external
and internal phenomena. This absence of a fixed or permanent
"thing" — a permanent, enduring "soul" — has profound ethical implications, above all that *we can grow.* Not being bound
by fixed and determinate identities, we have the capacity to
evolve, that is, to create and to re-create ourselves based on
wisdom and compassion. Buddhists hold that the misguided notion of a fixed, independent self issues in selfishness and, by
extension, in a whole host of strategies to support or maintain a certain self-concept or self-understanding. This program
issues in suffering, because we invariably find ourselves threatened in a world that insults our self-concepts. You're beautiful?
Age and illness will have something to say about that in the
long term. You're smart? Reality (and smarter people!) typically
reveals our limitations, as does the problem of cognitive de-
cline or, worse, dementia. Alzheimer's destroys the minds of the

brilliant, too. You're the best at what you do? Maybe. But certainly not always. Even the Yankees lose pennant races. You're a "good" person? Deep needs all too often painfully reveal the limitations of our moral capacities and the complexity of human experience.

The Teaching of Emptiness

The no-soul doctrine — "there is no person here" — is extended in later Buddhism to reflect the absence of "self" or "essence" in *anything*. And such absence is termed "emptiness." Although the word "emptiness" may carry negative emotional overtones for many of us — no one likes "feeling empty" — so to hear at first that emptiness is the truth of the universe may be bleak indeed. However, emptiness in Buddhism has rather precise technical valences. It indicates the absence of any decisive, defining mark or characteristic, one "findable" essence amid a constellation of events that we conventionally call a "thing." Emptiness means the impossibility of anything existing on its own terms, separate from a vast concatenation of relationships. Emptiness, in Buddhism, means relatedness. As applied to limited and "solid" notions of personal identity, the emptiness of self issues in a wider calibration of identity. To see only flow, one vastly intimate, intricate flow, changes everything. If there is no separation, no concrete, nail-down-able things out there, then there is only one embracing unity in which everything affects everything else; everything flows into everything else. No separation. Another way to put this is to say that if there is no "me" and if there is no "you," there is only *us*. This way of seeing has profound ethical — and even political — implications. For it means that we can no longer absolutize our "enemies" as "evil." They are complex, functioning out of competing psychological impulses as we do, too. Moreover, in this web of interrelationship, causal conditions reveal a more complex take on the enemy. In this view, overweening political or national self-centeredness breeds discord and resentment elsewhere. We, in part, by arrogance or selfishness writ large, help to create our "enemies." To meet the "enemy" with black and white assumptions is at the very least unproductive and ignores the host of complicated historical and political conditions that give rise to anger and hatred. The Dalai Lama is very clear about the need to be aware of such complexity in all contexts, including political. In the end, he writes, in harming the enemy, we harm ourselves, for negative consequences will ricochet back from political policies that demean, degrade, and harm others.

To see a recalibration of identity that shifts from standard self-centeredness to a broader dynamic inclusivity requires a training of the mind, one that subverts and transforms the standard conditioning of social and personal identity. In this sense, the philosophy of Buddhism in general, or emptiness doctrine more specifically, becomes a kind of cognitive and emotional therapy. And each impacts the other. The goal of Buddhist wisdom and meditation is to shape consciousness, above all to alter the structure of perception. This means that one does not merely assent to an intellectual understanding of reality, but actually perceives the world in accord with that understanding, that is, to "see" reality in this way. When one sees things rightly — sees the dissolution of self and concomitant web of interrelatedness — one cannot but express compassion. Because islands of self, barricaded by defense, dissolve in a greater web of relationship and connection. There's nothing to protect any longer; in fact, on this view there was never any self to protect in the first place. This recalibration of identity means seeing things as they are and finally realizing that "we're all in this together." Either we all go together to freedom, or none of us goes: the greater, more inclusive sense of identity means that there is no longer a distinction between "my" suffering and "your" suffering; there is just suffering. And the cardinal impulse of compassion always moves to mitigate suffering. The Dalai Lama takes as his daily aspiration this verse from the *Bodhicaryavatara* (Steps Leading to the Path of Enlightenment) of Shantideva, an eighth-century Indian monk:

> As long as space remains,
> As long as sentient beings remain,
> Until then, so too may I remain,
> And dispel the miseries of the world.

This is the commitment of the great archetypal hero in Buddhism, the Bodhisattva, the one who embodies wisdom and compassion and works tirelessly for the benefit of all sentient creatures. Shantideva notes that the hand of the body spontaneously moves to touch a scraped knee: it doesn't debate or consider pros and cons of doing so; it responds instinctively, effortlessly, and naturally. Similarly, the recalibration of identity means that all reality is our body, and, with right seeing, we similarly respond effortlessly and spontaneously to any harm to the greater body. This is one approach to cognitive therapy. If we retrain our way of seeing reality, less contention, competition, and conflict ensue. Our social world and personal worlds are no longer carved into bounded territories of "us" and "them." As the Dalai Lama and many others have noted, these contentious territories dissolve from a wider (and wiser) perspective. From space, one earth; no boundaries. As Stephen Batchelor notes, there are no lines in nature.[2] If not, what is there? A vast unity, a flow, a dance, an organic process.

---

2. Stephen Batchelor, *Buddhism without Beliefs: A Contemporary Guide to Awakening* (New York: Riverhead, 1977), 76.

Another approach to the cognitive transformation addresses the problem of language or "names." We might say that Buddhism is allergic to names. The reason for this recalls our grade school definitions of nouns: person, place, object, or thing. Nouns slow things down, solidify things, render concrete that which, for Buddhists, is not concrete. For Buddhists, reality is not a noun but a verb: moving, flowing, dancing. Names might be considered as a verbal analog to stop-action photography, which "locks" or freezes images in a single frame. For Buddhists, time-lapse photography more aptly reflect the way things are: flow. In this mode, reality is not frozen or locked, we don't "see" anything "solid" or nailed down, we see only flow and movement. Unfortunately, our standard perceptual program imputes solidity to that which is fluid and moving, not solid in any decisive, final way. We tend, according to the Sri Lankan monk Ananda Maitreya, "to see the solidity that is actually not there."[3]

In the area of language, names present the same problem as "stop-action" photography: while useful or beautiful or necessary, both give the wrong impression of reality. Names stop things, lock them down, render things solid, when there is nothing solid anywhere, but only movement and dance. Names improperly suggest a certain "findability" — the single decisive, definitive characteristic — but this "freezes" reality, concretizes it, fails to register the complex and rich weave of phenomena. The universe is a flowing mass of vibrations; how can we presume to select out certain data to name it in putatively final ways? At best we ought to do this with awareness of the limitations of names and definitions, a kind of necessary shorthand for conversation. But, according to Buddhist thought, we forget

---

3. *Footprint of the Buddha*, vol. 3 of *The Long Search Series*, 52 minutes, Time Life Video (distributed by Ambrose Video Publishing), 1977, videocassette.

that the names are shorthand and instead believe that they actually refer to real, isolated "things" out there. We then impute permanence to these "things" and layer them with emotional investments as objects to possess.

The name we give to a particular time-space slice is just that, a name. The technical definition for this important philosophical idea, one also seen in some Western schools of thought, is nominalism, "name only." For Buddhists, the name is a convenient fiction. Of course we must use names and categories for social interaction. Names facilitate expeditious communication. Nobody is going to articulate the endless stream of events and relationships that are found in the word "pencil": "Would you please pass the phenomena currently dancing with molecules of graphite and carbon, rubber and paint, fabricated from wood cut from a certain pine stand in a certain state, carted off by loggers, shipped by truckers to manufacturers, sold in bookstores everywhere but now here, in your hand?" Instead, we say, "Can I borrow a pencil?" So concepts or names are convenient tools for discourse. But, according to Buddhism, they are also fictions, and because we fail to see this, problems ensue: we impute permanence where there is no permanence. We "chunkify" the universe, as it were; that is, we populate it with "things" when, according to Buddhism, there are no "things" out there, only moving, flowing phenomena.

Names are illusory, not so much in the sense of being a mirage, but in the sense that names cannot capture a defining mark or characteristic of phenomena. So words are "unreal" or empty insofar as they are empty of a referent. A good example that illustrates how words can be empty of a referent may be found if a child asks if Martians are green. The question, of course, makes an assumption, namely, that there are Martians. But the word "Martian" has no referent; that is, there is nothing "out there" to which it refers. The word is empty. For

Buddhists, *all* words are like this. For social interaction we select or abstract from complex phenomena and "name" it. But
typically we tend to make that abstraction more real than the
phenomena from which it emerges. This process is called reifica-
tion or hypostatization or, perhaps more simply, concretization.
In the end, no one word can exhaustively pick out or isolate the
"thinghood" of a thing. Objects lack, according to the Dalai
Lama, a "findability," they are void of an essence or absolute,
final nature. Instead, objects are a mass of vibrations, dancing in
and with other vibrations; to recall again the Sri Lankan monk
Maitreya, "Apart from vibrations, there is nothing."[4]

For Buddhists, just as there are no things "out there," neither is
there anything "in here" as a permanent, decisive, final "thing."
No soul. No permanent, solid, substrate of personality. No permanent driver of the bus who pulls into the terminal (at death),
gets out, and looks for another "bus" or body. There is an amusing image in the film *Men in Black,* when an alien, who appears
to be human, lies dead in a morgue. One of the agents presses the
ear of the corpse, and a pneumatic release hisses, pops open the
"hood," so to speak, and behind the face is a tiny creature who
had been manipulating a host of levers and gears operating, as it
were, the human-like machine. The "inner alien" "driving" the
machine might be likened to a standard notion of soul, some independent entity, separate from the body, but nonetheless operating
the machine of our bodies. Buddhism rejects this assumption and
instead presses for a much more dynamic, integrated stream of
physical and mental events, including physical form, sensations,
ideas, tendencies, and consciousness. These are the so-called five
aggregates, which exhaustively account for what we call a person. None of these are permanent or unchanging, as we see in the
many changes that happen in each of these elements. But there is

---

4. Ibid.

a momentum, a movement to this system, one governed by the will to be a self. This movement, strong as it is, does not end at death but pushes forward, triggers another birth. But just as we are no longer the little baby we were years ago, but we are related — causally connected — to that baby, so too we will be related or causally connected to the new "person" whose birth was triggered by our stream of ethical and mental patterns and habits. In the end, whether "out there" as external objects or "in here" as mental processes, for Buddhists there are no enduring, permanent entities that somehow exist apart or above the phenomenal flow to which we give a name, "car," "book," "pencil," "you," "me." This is the key impulse of Buddhist wisdom, which the Dalai Lama unpacks repeatedly in his many books.

Morality

Ethical life is central to Buddhism. It follows wisdom and meditation but also precedes them as a necessary propaedeutic for mental purification. A typical human pattern is to act according to the strong emotions of desire (craving or greed) or anger (or hatred or hostility), and both of these operate from a fundamental misguided ignorance or delusion. Ignorance here is not some neutral nonknowing, but a kind of pro-active wrong headedness. The proactive misconception here is the notion of a self, which is the principal causal determinant of desire or hatred. That is, what we must have first in order to experience desire or feel pique is a particular self-concept. But from this sense of self comes selfishness and all the egocentric strategies marshaled to reinforce this particular concept. From "me" comes "mine" and all the limitations and tensions that follow. This sense of self is the cardinal delusion for Buddhists. In this view, we all conventionally function with a kind of low-level paranoia — not clinical, not nonfunctional, but an intense self-consciousness that is wary of how we "appear" and worries over the perceptions and judgments of others. Assuming a particular sense of self comes with strategies of reinforcement and defense and is marked by insecurity and anxiety in a competitive world in which everyone else is doing the same thing. The world then becomes threatening, unsafe. Our self-consciousness gets activated and we react in ways to defend, reinforce, or restore our sense of self.

Ethical life is important because it begins to act on or express wisdom in constructive, wholesome, appropriate ways. It begins the process of rewiring the circuitry of our minds by opening up new patterns, creating new habits, and "short-circuiting," as it were, habituated patterns governed by reactivity and selfishness. This is done with particular vigor in and through meditation, but ethical behavior contributes to mental purification. Meditation and action are on the same continuum of mental operation, because all action contains a mental overlay: intention. Two verses from the *Dhammapada* reflect this, and the first begins the text: "What we are today comes from our thoughts of yesterday, and our present thoughts build our life tomorrow: our life is the creation of our mind."[5] This is not to imply a philosophical idealism, but to make the observation that our life is the result of our will, habits, and intentions, and these emerge from our mind. If this is the case, and if we find ourselves suffering from particular circumstances, the counsel of course would then be: change your mind. Assert resolve and intention toward wholesome outcomes, then carry these forth in action. A famous verse in the *Dhammapada* "condenses" Buddhism, as it were: "Do good, avoid evil, purification of the mind. This is the

5. *The Dhammapada*, trans. Juan Mascaro (New York: Penguin Books, 1973), 35.

teaching of all the Buddhas."[6] Here we see the mental continuum: action is on the same plane as mental purification. Ethical programs begin to clear the mind of "afflictive" emotions — desire and anger — so called because they cause affliction: they hurt ourselves and others. The first fruit of this process is a life free of anxiety and marked by calm and contentment. And, with a mind unclouded by roaring emotional impulses, one is better equipped to meditate and extend this process of transformation.

We can take several approaches to consider the importance of ethics. The first builds from the above notions. The standard ethical program in Buddhism begins with following the five precepts: not to kill, not to steal, not to lie, not to engage in sexual impropriety, not to drink intoxicants. These are precepts, not commandments. They are not absolutes to measure ourselves by, and by which we inevitably fall short, but they are great "undertakings," marking a particular way or orientation in the world. When we do "miss the mark," the objective is to forgive ourselves and others, resolve again, carry on. The goal here is not to strain to some ideal of perfection, which in the end is burdensome and alienating. In fact, the old adage is tweaked: it's not so much that practice makes perfect, but that in the practice is perfection. The practice of these virtues instantiates the goal itself: the embodiment of wisdom and compassion, the embodiment of selflessness. The five precepts are common to Indian religious traditions — we see versions of them in the Yoga Sutra and in the Jain traditions, not to mention keen parallels in other religions traditions. We can easily account for such universality. If we live in a human skin, whether we are from Boise or Bangkok, we notice that minds in the grip of craving and

---

6. *Footprint of the Buddha*. Also, rendered slightly differently, in Mascaro, *Dhammapada*, 62.

aversion are not calm, have very little perspective, tend to tele-
scope into self-centeredness, and this in the end typically causes
trouble. Undertaking these precepts begins to calm the mind,
cultivates a wider perspective, opens up constricted hearts. For
the Dalai Lama, ethics is the supremely universal dynamic in
the religions of the world. As he writes in *Ethics for a New Millennium,* altruism is his religion. While this may indeed be so,
it is important to bear in mind the metaphysical structure that
frames and calls forth these ethical principles. Metaphysics generates ethics. That is, how we understand reality directly leads
to ethical choices. And the central metaphysic in Buddhism is
the absence of separate, isolatable "selves." This is emptiness.

The five precepts, articulated as restraints upon behavior, are
set in a wider context of "right speech" and "right livelihood,"
two of the key prescriptions in the eightfold path, "right"
here having little to do with absolute standards but instead in-
volving a lifestyle that cultivates wholesome mental states and
erodes unwholesome states. For example, we need little analysis
to identify "wrong" speech: corrosive, demeaning, or insulting
words; lying; backbiting or gossip. All of these patterns cause
harm: certainly to the person to whom these patterns are directed but, in the end, to the person directing them too, for
negative consequences typically follow unrestrained and hurt-
ful speech. These could include losing one's job, as has been the
case with some television and radio personalities, or it could
mean experiencing a self-caused alienation. Many people do not
find it particularly healthy to associate with mean-spirited persons, and the latter may find themselves quite alone owing to
the consequences of their behavior.

According to Buddhism, all unskillful behavior emerges from
a central "delusion" or ignorance or misguided premise: the
sense of "self." The sense of "me," inflated and demanding,
asserts itself in competition and contention over and against

another, "you." But this spells suffering for both parties. This happens in "wrong speech" but we see it easily in "wrong action," too. Beginning from a misguided sense of self, unrestrained anger can lead to injury or worse, once again harming not only the object of anger but its subject, too. While the harm to another may be obvious, it also harms the subject. This is made clear by the consequences of anger and hostility. There is a famous maxim of the Buddha: "You are not punished for your anger. You are punished by your anger." While anger may sometimes be clarifying and perhaps even justified, most of us do not feel very content or peaceful when angry. Because it saps our peace and contentment, anger is an "afflictive" emotion, i.e., it causes affliction or suffering. Moreover, anger too easily issues in an exercise of ego and power, and "righteous" anger slips into self-righteousness. With respect to the practice of nonviolence, an awareness of the existential plight of all creatures calls forth sensitivity and compassion leading to restraint of violent impulses. In the *Dhammapada*, we read, "All beings tremble before danger, all fear death. Knowing this, one does not kill or cause to kill."[7]

Buddhist ethics are comprehended in a positive construction of virtues as well. In the Buddhist view, there are six (or ten, depending on the tradition) classic virtues cultivated in lifetime after lifetime: generosity, morality, forbearance, effort, meditation, and wisdom. Wisdom — seeing reality as a great web of connection — in fact informs all the virtues. And generosity, truly a premier virtue here, is important because it instantiates selflessness. When we give something of value to another, we are not thinking about our needs or our attachments or the sense of *our* identity that is emotionally layered into the object; in thinking of the other, we let go. We discover that we

---

7. *The Dhammapada*, 54. I slightly modified Mascaro's translation.

are not defined by the object (or person); we may suffer a sting
of loss, but we learn that, as with everything, the sting passes.
Stepping aside from our own personal investment in the object,
we may also discover that joy we experience when we see the
impact of our generosity on another. This is not to create yet
another egotistical self-construction, "I am a generous person,"
but simply to note the constructive impact of selfless actions
both on the other and on ourselves. Indeed, the Dalai Lama
sometimes speaks of "wise selfishness," by which he means, at
a conventional level, we do recognize that our thoughtful actions help another, but they offer something to us, too, a sense
of joy or peace or satisfaction in knowing we've done or tried
to do something beneficial for another.

The Teaching of Cause and Effect

There are other approaches to ethics, once again germinat-
ing from metaphysics. The principle of interdependence can be
viewed in a particular time-slice matrix — say, for example,
"Tom" — and it can be viewed from a broader cosmic perspective. In the former, Buddhism might counsel bearing close
scrutiny on our lives, seeing the unfathomably rich and mysterious impact of cause and effect on our lives. We can stand
toward the past and see the intricate weave of our lives — its
sequences and patterns in our personal, family, social, and religious histories. At the same time we see the impact of this
complex weave in our relationships, above all, the manner in
which we benefited from the kindness of others and caused
benefit to others, and the manner in which we were hurt by
others and also hurt others. We see these consequences and
recognize an obvious truth: peace and joy follow from wholesome choices and distress and harm follow from unwholesome
choices. Buddhism asks us to take a good look at our lives, say

"yes" to it all, accept it, integrate, learn from it, especially the principle of cause and effect. We are "here" because of a sequence of cause and effect, the consequence of unfathomably rich patterns of choices we've made and choices visited upon us. Concerning the latter, if, for example, one's mother seriously abused alcohol during pregnancy, it is highly dubious that that person would be reading this book, given the deleterious effects of fetal alcohol syndrome on cognition. In this case, a certain life trajectory already becomes established in the womb. However, many of us have been raised in nurturing households — with requisite doses of neurosis (this must be admitted too) — that cultivated a set of life skills, the value of education, various moral and spiritual sensibilities, and our own particular curriculum of gift, heartache, and loss. Buddhism says be aware of it all, above all the impact of cause and effect. Now look to the future. Knowing what peace and suffering feel like and knowing the consequences of actions, "you" at this time are ethically obligated to establish wholesome conditions for the benefit of "you" in the future. While you are no longer that bouncing bundle of baby fat, you are causally connected to that baby; similarly, you are also causally related to the "new" incarnation of "you" ten minutes from now, ten years from now, thirty years from now. At the same time, not only does ethical practice benefit "you-in-the-future," it also benefits "you-now," for the practice contains the goal right here and now. Moreover, our actions now also ripple forth, like a rock dropped in the middle of the pond whose waves ripple to the banks. As such, our actions impact others. The prescription? Be mindful of our actions.

The patterns of cause and effect in our lives are like great and little reverberations. Actions ripple forth with their consequences, sometimes in devastating ways. A child who was physically or sexually abused suffers ongoing emotional trauma, which becomes a tidal wave of damage. Natural catastrophic events also vividly demonstrate the force and damage of reverberating impact, in addition to the constructive impulse in the face of it. In 2004, converging plate boundaries in the Pacific shifted due to an earthquake. The resulting tectonic shift caused not mere ripples but cascading tidal waves racing across the globe at jet speed. The tsunami devastated countries in Southeast Asia, South Asia, and Africa, claiming over two hundred thousand lives. At the same time, precisely owing to the increasingly tight and interconnected global "weave," news of the devastating event cascaded forth in every form of media. The vivid transmission of catastrophic suffering stimulated a cardinal human impulse, compassion, and millions of people sent funds, assistance, labor, materials to the afflicted countries. Many people in America went straight to the local Wal-Mart, bought medicines and clothes, boxed them, and delivered them to relief organizations. The tectonic "reverb" was thus met with a reverb of compassion. Similarly, in our lives, even the unwholesome or unconstructive choices issuing from tectonic shifts of psyche can be redeemed by the choices for compassion, kindness, and generosity.

Another example illustrates the evolutionary program presupposed in the principle of cause and effect. In this case, we might consider the astonishing and impossible array of events that lead to us being here. Consider the solar system. The solar system was forged nearly five billion years ago by the imploding death of a star. That dying star sent heavy molecules exploding forth; these, gradually, condensed and formed our solar system, and, in an impossibly thin frame of causality, generated the precise conditions to allow life on earth to develop, beginning the process of evolution. This intricate, tender, and sure process unfolded in due course, with plant and animal species developing, and in time civilizations, and finally our own local histories with ancestries from different parts of the world and eventually our own personal histories. Think of it this way: the entire universe has dovetailed in unfathomably subtle ways to impact you, to create you. If the universe impacts you, you in turn impact the universe. As a rock dropped in the middle of the pond ripples forth its waves, so our actions ripple forth affecting both ourselves and others. It is therefore incumbent to act ethically.

Meditation

Meditation is the process of transforming consciousness, to see reality as it is. This means we have to rewire the circuitry, as it were. Our minds become grooved or encoded with patterned or habituated responses to stimuli. If we respond the same way to the same stimuli over time, we now have a habit or tendency. The problem is that this habit tends to become our "automatic default." In the presence of certain conditions, we slip into the default. The inability to act autonomously in these situations — reacting instead of acting — means that we really aren't "lords" of ourselves. We slip into knee-jerk reactions. We aren't in control. This typically causes problems for ourselves and for others. The Dalai Lama's discussion of meditation in his books is sophisticated and rich and reveals the intimate relationship that obtains between wisdom, ethics, and meditation.

While there are over forty different kinds of meditation in the Buddhist tradition, all of them can be grouped generally by the last two steps of the eightfold path: right mindfulness and right concentration. Right mindfulness involves bringing awareness to each phenomenal event, beginning with sensations in the body as one breathes and walks. This same kind of awareness can be directed to the mind, as one develops his or her passive and nonjudgmental awareness. This develops an emotional distance between the mental event and the observer, so that the observer does not automatically slip into habituated patterns of reactivity. Merely to observe, "This is an instance of fear" or "This is an instance of anger," asserts an authority over fear and anger, rather than becoming victim to them. Mindfulness meditation in the end helps to cultivate calm (*shamatha*), and while Buddhist tradition does not hold that this state itself is nirvana, it is an important step in the program of liberation, for without a mind whose emotions are under control, we cannot look critically into the deeper structure of reality. We cannot hope to see reality as it is when our minds rampage like a wild elephant, as the Dalai Lama says. The mind needs to be calm. Such calm is also cultivated by the practice of morality and virtue, especially generosity. Indeed, the outcome of a moral life is not only a presumed increased ability to meditate; it is also a life free from anxiety and contention, a life marked with peace and contentment. While such a state may not be nirvana, it is nonetheless compelling and indicates the real world benefits of spiritual practice.

More intensified programs of meditation are grouped, generally, under the rubric of right concentration or, elsewhere, the cultivation of insight (*vipashyana bhavana*). In this case meditation is no longer passive or mere bare awareness but instead is manipulative and analytical. That is, in this case, the meditator actively engages the content of Buddhist teaching — the four Noble Truths, the five aggregates, dependent origination — and "works it" mentally. This analytical program deconstructs false notions of self or world as anything concrete or fixed or stable. It drives home, as it were, the truth of impermanence and reveals the fluid, interconnected dynamic of phenomenal reality. Analytical meditations technically draw upon the content of Buddhist doctrine to provoke such insight, or they may even use other devices — such as "disgusting" meditations on the varying stages of decomposition of a corpse — to trigger it. In any case, the operative approach is active and analytical. In this collection, the Dalai Lama categorizes the two general approaches as "settled" and "analytical," and the latter may sometimes also involve an intense examination of the untoward effects of afflictive emotions in order to see clearly their destructive impact. Seeing clearly, one resolves not to accommodate them and instead to cultivate their opposite, namely, patience and kindness. Hence, meditation in this case is stimulated by wisdom and ends in morality.

One of the most famous meditations in the Buddhist tradition is the meditation on loving-kindness. I mention it here and I include the Dalai Lama's representation of it in the book because it is so central to Buddhist spirituality; moreover, it is a method that easily crosses cultural and religious boundaries. The premise of the loving-kindness meditation is that every person deserves happiness and freedom from suffering. All have a birthright to happiness. And there is no one who deserves it more than the meditator, and this is how the meditation begins. One mentally showers oneself with loving-kindness, perhaps envisioning holding oneself as an infant. The psychological insight is astute. We must love ourselves before we love others, otherwise the manner of our moving through the world will be marked by an excessive dependency on others for validation and approval.

The meditation then extends to a loved one, a neutral person (say, the woman working the cash register at the grocery store), a benefactor, and, when possible, the "difficult" one, the person or persons in our lives who are genuinely problematic for us as we try to work with them — or perhaps even live with them! (Surely parents are the "difficult ones" for adolescents — and vice versa!) And, while there may be someone in our lives

who is difficult for us, admittedly we may be challenging for
him or her, too. But this is the nature of the real world; there
is no pie-in-the-sky otherworldly sensibility here. We are limited. But the difficult ones become great teachers for us, for they
stretch our capacities for patience, generosity, and compassion.
The truth is, again, every person on the planet and every person
in our lives deserves to be happy. The difficult one no less than
anyone else.

A Final Note

I have included representative selections on wisdom, morality,
and meditation from the many books by the Dalai Lama, and
in doing so I have tried to keep in mind what might be most
helpful to the general reader. As will be evident in reading the
book, wisdom, morality, and meditation are always closely in-
tertwined, so elements of each, particularly wisdom, may be
found in each section. Additionally, I've tried to strike a balance
between short, pithy, almost aphoristic statements of the Dalai
Lama and more extended discussion of a topic. The former
offer memorable observations or maxims and become rich, if
brief, thoughts for consideration. Longer passages often represent an extended explication of Buddhist content. The teaching
of Buddhism is sophisticated and highly developed, and even in
a general representation such as this, one cannot and ought not
to avoid some of the more complicated philosophy. It would
honor neither the depth of Buddhism nor the Dalai Lama himself if the texts remained only at a rudimentary level. The Dalai
Lama is an excellent teacher, and I've often found his explanations to be lucid, cogent, and illustrative. The texts stand for
themselves. Hopefully, this introduction helps to set the stage
for some of his discussion and can be used to refer back, as

needed, for clarification of the general content of Buddhist philosophy. A final chapter includes texts on a variety of topics: the Dalai Lama's understanding of religion and religious pluralism, science and spirituality, and fundamental global concerns. Even here philosophical perspectives are never far from the surface, and this is not surprising, since philosophy in Buddhism informs the whole of our lives, including what we see and how we choose to live.

1

Wisdom

The Dalai Lama's intense training in Buddhist philosophy is remarkable given the unstable political climate in which he was raised. Despite the initial invasion of Tibet by China in 1950, the Dalai Lama continued to master the complexities of Buddhist doctrine, especially the Madhyamaka (Middle Way) philosophy of the great second-century monk Nagarjuna and the vast scripture called Prajnaparamita, *the perfection of wisdom literature. Both resources explore the central doctrine of emptiness, a complex notion that the Dalai Lama lucidly explains here. The doctrine of emptiness, rather than indicating some bleak nothingness, in the end signals the interrelatedness of all phenomenal events. This vast perspective offers great emotional space for understanding others, even those whom we might call our "enemies." We see, then, a cardinal instinct in Buddhism. Wisdom, that is, the capacity to see things rightly, leads to compassion. Metaphysics leads to morality. This chapter focuses on metaphysics, including theoretical and practical wisdom, and the following chapter addresses morality.*

In the summer of 1958, the Dalai Lama engaged the first battery of examinations of his academic training. This included intense debates with scholars from the two great monastic centers near Lhasa, Sera and Drepung. He passed these exams and was told that if he'd had the same study opportunities as an ordinary monk, his effort would have been unsurpassed. With typical humility, the Dalai Lama writes in his autobiography, "So I felt very happy that this lazy student did not in the end disgrace himself."[1]

In early March of 1959, prior to his escape to India, he completed the final phase of his examination, debates before an audience of thousands of people. After an intense, exhausting day of oral examination, he was unanimously awarded the geshe degree, the Tibetan equivalent of a Ph.D. in Buddhist studies. On March 17, after a failed uprising in Lhasa and increasing political tension with the Chinese, he began his escape to India. In this we might say his scholarly training in the subtleties of Buddhist philosophy met the ultimate test in the real-world encounter with violence and oppression. In Buddhist thought, wisdom is never abstract but always moves to practical application. Wisdom sees things rightly: the absence of any final, defining quality to phenomenal events. This means, for example, the "enemy" is not something fixed or concrete. The so-called "enemy" cannot be objectified or demonized. Because of this, the Dalai Lama has practiced a meditation in which he visualizes absorbing the hatred and animosity of the Chinese and extends, instead, compassion. Why? Genuine love is unconditional, not predicated on the other's behavior or favors to us. In the Dalai Lama's meditation, Buddhist "theory" meets practice. Wisdom becomes compassion.

---

1. The Dalai Lama, *Freedom in Exile* (New York: HarperCollins, 1990), 129.

PREMISES

Developing wisdom is a process of bringing our minds into accordance with the way things are.   —*An Open Heart*, 86

We can never obtain peace in the world if we neglect the inner world and don't make peace with ourselves.
                                           —*A Policy of Kindness*, 95

AN ANTHROPOLOGY

We are all children of the one human race. We all bear the same longing for happiness and love within us. We all want to reduce suffering. We all know how important a good heart is.

   This is a heart full of kindness, compassion, and love — from which hope and inner peace flow. So I believe that a good heart is ultimately the root and source for genuine progress. Especially today, universal responsibility, which is based on love and kindness, has become for humanity a question of survival.
                                  —*Path of Wisdom, Path of Peace*, 78

The basic fact is that all sentient beings, particularly human beings, want happiness and do not want pain and suffering. On those grounds, we have every right to be happy and to use different methods or means to overcome suffering and to achieve happier lives. These methods, however, should not infringe on the rights of others, nor should they create more suffering for others. It is worthwhile to think seriously about the positive and negative consequences of these methods. You should be aware that there are differences between short-term and long-term interests and consequences. If there is a conflict between the short-term interest and the long-term interest, the long-term

interest is more important. Buddhists usually say that there is
no absolute and that everything is relative. So we must judge
according to the circumstances.

— *The Power of Compassion*, 2

One of my fundamental convictions is that basic human nature is more disposed toward compassion and affection. Basic
human nature is gentle, not aggressive or violent....I would
also argue that when we examine the relationship between
mind or consciousness, and body, we see that wholesome attitudes, emotions, and states of mind, like compassion, tolerance,
and forgiveness, are strongly connected with physical health
and well-being, whereas negative or unwholesome attitudes and
emotions — anger, hatred, disturbed states of mind — undermine physical health. I would argue that this correspondence
shows that our basic human nature is closer to the wholesome
attitudes and emotions.   — *The Good Heart*, 50

All things have two sides. This is true of the human self as
well. There is the egotistical self that constantly inflates itself
and becomes a disastrous troublemaker. And when individuals
inconsiderately assert themselves because of ego addiction, they
hurt not only others but themselves. This self causes suffering.
Then there is the self of the will, which lets people say: "I can,
I must, I want."

When this center of the will is lacking, a person cannot deal
with negative aspects, such as anger, envy, or hatred, and instead is overwhelmed by them. Our sensations and feelings react
spontaneously. We want to possess something or we reject it.
Only a strongly developed will can manage the various feelings.

— *Path of Wisdom, Path of Peace*, 54–55

If we examine the nature of suffering, we will find that there are certain types of suffering that are amenable to solutions and can thus be overcome. Once we realize this, we should seek their solution and the means to overcome the suffering. But there are also other types of suffering that are inevitable and insurmountable. In such cases, it is important to develop a state of mind that will allow you to deal with this suffering in a realistic way. By doing so, you may be able to accept these difficulties as they arise. Such an attitude will protect you, not necessarily from the physical reality of suffering, but from the unnecessary, added psychological burden of struggling against the suffering.

—*The Good Heart*, 54

Our attitude toward suffering becomes very important because it can affect how we cope with suffering when it arises. Now, our usual attitude consists of an intense aversion and intolerance of our pain and suffering. *However, if we can transform our attitude toward suffering, adopt an attitude that allows us greater tolerance of it, then this can do much to help counteract feelings of mental unhappiness, dissatisfaction, and discontent....*

I think that how you perceive life as a whole plays a role in your attitude about suffering. For instance, if your basic outlook is that suffering is negative and must be avoided at all costs and in some sense is a sign of failure, this will add a distinct psychological component of anxiety and intolerance when you encounter difficult circumstances, a feeling of being overwhelmed. On the other hand, if your basic outlook accepts that suffering is a natural part of your existence, this will undoubtedly make you more tolerant toward the adversities of life. —*Art of Happiness*, 140–41

*We also often add to our pain and suffering by being overly
sensitive, overreacting to minor things, and sometimes taking
things too personally.*   — Art of Happiness, 152

INTERDEPENDENCE

Since our very existence and well-being are a result of the cooperation and contributions of countless others, we must develop
a proper attitude about the way we relate to them. We often
tend to forget this basic fact. Today, in our modern global econ-
omy, national boundaries are irrelevant. Not only do countries
depend upon one another, but so do continents. We are heavily
interdependent....

If we looked down at the world from space, we would not
see any demarcations of national boundaries. We would simply see one small planet, just one. Once we draw a line in the
sand, we develop the feeling of "us" and "them." As this feeling
grows, it becomes harder to see the reality of the situation....

In a sense the concept of "us" and "them" is almost no
longer relevant, as our neighbors' interests are ours as well. Caring for our neighbors' interests is essentially caring for our own
future. Today the reality is simple. In harming our enemy, we
are harmed.   — An Open Heart, 9–10

I would like to point out a particular element in the practice of
the Bodhisattva path that might be suitable for a Christian to
practice. There is a special category of teachings and practices
known as *lo jong:* thought transformation, or mind training.
There is a special way of reflecting upon the kindness of all sentient beings, in this context all human beings, that is described
in some of the literature. For example, we can easily perceive
the kindness of someone who is directly involved in our life and

our upbringing. But if you examine the nature of your existence, including your physical survival, you will find that all the factors that contribute to your existence and well-being — such as food, shelter, and even fame — come into being only through the cooperation of other people.

This is especially true in the case of someone who lives an urban life. Almost every aspect of your life is heavily dependent upon others. For example, if there is an electricians' strike for even just one day, our whole city comes to a halt. This heavy interdependency upon others' cooperation is so obvious that no one needs to point it out. This is also true of your food and shelter. You need the direct or indirect cooperation of many people to make these necessities available. Even for such an ephemeral phenomenon as fame you need others. If you live alone in a mountainous wilderness, the only thing close to fame that you could create would be an echo! Without other people, there is no possibility of creating fame. So in almost every aspect of your life there is the participation and involvement of other people.

If you think along these lines, you will begin to recognize the kindness of others. And if you are a spiritual practitioner, you will also be aware that all of the major spiritual traditions of the world recognize the preciousness of altruism and compassion. If you examine this precious mind or emotion of altruism, of compassion, you will see that you need an object to generate even this feeling. And that object is a fellow human being. From this point of view, that very precious state of mind, compassion, is impossible without the presence of others. Every aspect of your life — your religious practice, your spiritual growth, even your basic survival — is impossible without others. When you think along such lines, you will find sufficient grounds to feel connected with others, to feel the need to repay their kindness.

In light of these convictions, it becomes impossible to believe that some people are totally irrelevant to your life or that you can afford to adopt an indifferent attitude toward them. There are no human beings who are irrelevant to your life.

—The Good Heart, 69–70

THE AWARENESS OF CAUSE AND EFFECT FOR MENTAL TRANSFORMATION

In Buddhism we talk of two types of causes. First, there are the substantial ones. In the metaphor [of seed], this would consist of the seed, which, with the cooperation of certain conditions, generates an effect that is in its own natural continuum, i.e., the sprout. The conditions that enable the seed to generate this sprout — water, sunlight, soil, and fertilizers — would be considered that sprout's cooperative causes or conditions. That things arise in dependence upon causes and conditions, whether substantial or cooperative, is not because of the force of people's actions or because of the extraordinary qualities of the Buddha. It is simply the way things are....

Though not physical, our states of mind also come about by causes and conditions, much the way things in the physical world do. It is therefore important to develop familiarity with the mechanics of causation. The substantial cause of our present state of mind is the previous moment of mind. Thus, each moment of consciousness serves as the substantial cause of our subsequent awareness. The stimuli experienced by us, visual forms we enjoy or memories we react to, are the cooperative conditions that give our state of mind its character. As with matter, by controlling the conditions, we affect the product: our mind. Meditation should be a skillful method of doing just this, applying particular conditions to our minds in order to bring about the desired effect, a more virtuous mind....

Analytical meditation is the process of carefully applying and cultivating particular thoughts that enhance positive states of mind and diminish and ultimately eliminate negative ones. This is how the mechanism of cause and effect is utilized constructively....

It is only by our concerted effort, an effort based on an understanding of how the mind and its various emotional and psychological states interact, that we bring about true spiritual progress. If we wish to lessen the power of negative emotions, we must search for the causes that give rise to them. We must work at removing or uprooting those causes. At the same time, we must enhance the mental forces that counter them: what we might call their antidotes. This is how a meditator must gradually bring about the mental transformation he or she seeks....

When we recognize how our thoughts have particular effects upon our psychological states, we can prepare ourselves for them. We will then know that when one state of mind arises, we must counter it in a particular way; and if another occurs, we must act appropriately. When we see our mind drifting toward angry thoughts of someone we dislike, we must catch ourselves; we must change our mind by changing the subject. It is difficult to hold back from anger when provoked unless we have trained our mind to first recollect the unpleasant effects such thoughts will cause us. It is therefore essential that we begin our training in patience calmly, not while we are experiencing anger. We must recall in detail how, when angry, we lose our peace of mind, how we are unable to concentrate on our work, and how unpleasant we become to those around us. It is by thinking long and hard in this manner that we eventually become able to refrain from anger. — *An Open Heart*, 58–62

THE TRUTH OF NO FIXED IDENTITIES AND ITS IMPLICATIONS

Ultimately, all our difficulties arise from one basic illusion. We believe in the inherent existence of ourselves and all other phenomena. We project, and then cling to, an idea of the intrinsic nature of things, an essence that phenomena do not actually possess. Let us take a simple chair as an example. We believe, without fully recognizing this belief, that there is such a thing as an essential chair-ness, a quality of a chair that seems to exist among its parts: the legs, seat, and back. In the same way, we each believe there to be an essential and continuous "me" pervading the physical and mental parts that make up each of us; it does not actually exist.

Our grasping at this inherent existence is a fundamentally mistaken perception that we must eliminate through meditation practices of the wisdom path. Why? Because it is the root cause of all our misery. It lies at the core of all our afflictive emotions.

We can abandon this illusion of an essential quality only by cultivating its direct antidote, which is the wisdom that realizes the nonexistence of that quality. Again, we cultivate this profound wisdom, as we cultivate humility to uproot pride. We must first become aware of the improper way we perceive ourselves and other phenomena; we can then cultivate a correct perception of phenomena.... By directly realizing our lack of an inherent nature, we uproot the very basis of self-grasping that lies at the core of all our suffering.   — *An Open Heart*, 85–86

What is the value of these observations? They have a number of important implications. Firstly, when we come to see that everything we perceive and experience arises as a result of an indefinite series of interrelated causes and conditions, our whole perspective changes. We begin to see that the universe we inhabit can be understood in terms of a living organism where each cell works in balanced cooperation with every other cell to sustain the whole. If, then, just one of these cells is harmed, as when disease strikes, that balance is harmed and there is danger to the whole. This, in turn, suggests that our individual well-being is intimately connected both with that of all others and with the environment within which we live. It also becomes apparent that our every action, our every deed, word, and thought, no matter how slight or inconsequential it may seem, has an implication not only for ourselves but for all others, too.

Furthermore, when we view reality in terms of dependent origination, it draws us away from our usual tendency to see things and events in terms of solid, independent, discrete entities. This is helpful because it is this tendency which causes us to exaggerate one or two aspects of our experience and make them representative of the whole reality of a given situation while ignoring its wider complexities.

Such an understanding of reality as suggested by this concept of dependent origination also presents us with a significant challenge. It challenges us to see things and events less in terms of black and white and more in terms of a complex interlinking of relationships, which are hard to pin down. And it makes it difficult to speak in terms of absolutes. Moreover, if all phenomena are dependent on other phenomena, and if no phenomena can exist independently, even our most cherished selves must be considered not to exist in the way we normally assume. Indeed, we find that if we search for the identity of the self analytically, its apparent solidity dissolves even more readily than that of the clay pot or the present moment [which rapidly dissolves into the past]. For whereas a pot is something concrete we can actually point to, the self is more elusive: its identity as a construct quickly becomes evident. We come to see that the habitual sharp designation we make between "self" and "others" is an exaggeration. —*Ethics for the New Millennium*, 40–42

The "identitylessness" of phenomena points rather to the way in which things exist: not independently but in a sense interdependently. —*Ethics for the New Millennium*, 45

If the self had intrinsic identity, it would be possible to speak in terms of self-interest in isolation from that of others. But because this is not so, because self and others can only be understood in terms of relationship, we see that self-interest and others' interest are closely interrelated. Indeed, within this picture of dependently originated reality, we see that there is no self-interest completely unrelated to others' interests. Due to the fundamental interconnectedness which lies at the heart of reality, your interest is also my interest. From this it becomes clear that "my" interest and "your" interest are intimately connected. In a deep sense, they converge. —*Ethics for the New Millennium*, 47

If we examine our emotions, our experiences of powerful attachment or hostility, we find that at their root is an intense clinging to a concept of self. Such a self we assume to be independent and self-sufficient, with a solid reality. As our belief in this kind of self intensifies, so does our wish to satisfy and protect it.

Let me give you an example. When you see a beautiful watch in a shop, you are naturally attracted to it. If the salesperson were to drop the watch, you would think, "Oh dear, the watch has fallen." The impact on you would not be very great. If, however, you bought the watch and have come to think of it as "my watch," then, were you to drop it, the impact would be devastating. You would feel as if your heart were jumping out of you. Where does this powerful feeling come from? Possessiveness arises out of our sense of self. The stronger our sense of "me," the stronger is our sense of "mine." This is why it is so important that we work at undercutting our belief in an independent, self-sufficient self. Once we are able to question and dissolve the existence of such a concept of self, the emotions derived from it are also diminished.   —*An Open Heart*, 152

Through the twelve links of dependent origination, Buddha teaches that all things and all events, including all elements of one's individual experience, come into being merely as a result of the aggregation of causes and conditions. Understanding this, in turn, can lead us to see that all things are by nature interdependent, originating entirely as a result of other things and other factors.

Buddha teaches that the very fact that something is dependently originated means that it is necessarily devoid of an essential, or independent, reality. For if something is fundamentally *dependent*, by logical necessity it must be devoid of having a nature that is independent of other phenomena, of existing *independently*. Thus it is said that anything that is dependently originated must also be, in actual fact, empty.

—*Essence of the Heart Sutra*, 30

EMPTINESS

So what is emptiness? It is simply this unfindability (the absence of an intrinsic, independent, self-existing reality). When we look for the flower among its parts, we are confronted with the absence of such a flower. That absence we are confronted with is the flower's emptiness. But then, is there no flower? Of course there is. To seek for the core of any phenomenon is ultimately to arrive at a more subtle appreciation of its emptiness, its un-findability. However, we mustn't think about the emptiness of a flower simply as the unfindability we encounter when searching among its parts. Rather, it is the dependent nature of the flower, or whatever object you care to name, that defines its emptiness. This is called dependent origination.

The notion of dependent origination is explained in various ways by different Buddhist philosophers. Some define it merely in relation to the laws of causation. They explain that such a thing as a flower is the product of causes and conditions; it arises dependently. Others interpret dependence more subtly. For them, a phenomenon is dependent when it depends on its parts, the way our flower depends upon its petals, stamen, and pistil.

There is an even more subtle interpretation of dependent origination. Within the context of a single phenomenon like the flower, its parts — the petals, stamen, and pistil — and our thought recognizing or naming the flower are mutually dependent. One cannot exist without the other. Therefore, when analyzing or searching for a flower among its parts, you will not find it. And yet, the perception of a flower exists only in relation to the parts that make it up. From this understanding of dependent origination ensues a rejection of any idea of intrinsic or inherent existence.   *— An Open Heart*, 154–55

The meaning of Emptiness is the interdependent nature of reality.   *— Power of Compassion*, 103

Accepting a more complex understanding of reality where all things and events are seen to be closely interrelated does not mean we cannot infer that the ethical principles we identified earlier cannot be understood as binding, even if, on this view, it becomes difficult to speak in terms of absolutes, at least outside a religious context. On the contrary, the concept of dependent origination compels us to take the reality of cause and effect with utmost seriousness. By this I mean the fact that particular causes lead to particular effects, and that certain actions lead to suffering while others lead to happiness. It is in everybody's interest to do what leads to happiness and avoid that which leads to suffering. But because, as we have seen, our interests are inextricably linked, we are compelled to accept ethics as the indispensable interface between my desire to be happy and yours. — *Ethics for the New Millennium*, 47

I think it would be useful to reflect on a fundamental metaphysical view in Buddhist philosophy, the doctrine of emptiness. In essence, this says that the fact that things exist is very obvious and apparent; our experience of interacting with physical reality and matter is sufficient evidence for us to accept this. The question is, in what manner do they exist?

Upon examining the ultimate nature of reality, Buddhist philosophers have concluded that things lack inherent existence, that is, they do not have self-defining, self-evident characteristics. This is because if we search for the essence of matter in whatever object it may be, we discover that it is unfindable, and when we subject things to ultimate analysis, we find that they do not exist as they appear to. Therefore, by subjecting the nature of reality to such analysis, we find that things do not have the solid, objective reality that they appear to have, that there is a discrepancy between the way things appear and the way in which they exist. This conclusion prevents us from falling into the extreme of absolutism, from holding on to some kind of absolutist view of reality. At the same time, because our empirical experience validates the existence of phenomena and is all the evidence we need that things exist, we cannot deny the nominal existence of things. This frees us from falling into the extreme of nihilism.

The question then arises, if things neither exist as they appear nor possess this objective reality, while at the same time they do exist, what then is their mode of existence? Buddhism explains that they exist only conventionally, in relative terms.

— *MindScience*, 23–24

Emptiness is the ultimate nature of reality in the sense that it is the mere absence of the inherent nature, or reified projection, that we impute on reality.   — *MindScience*, 25

The reason why it is so important to understand this subtle point [emptiness] is because of its implications for interpreting our own personal experience of life. When strong emotions arise in you, say attachment or anger, if you examine the experience of that emotion you will see that underlying it is an assumption that there is something objective and real out there which you are holding on to, and on to which you project desirable or undesirable qualities. According to the kind of qualities you project on to a thing or event, you feel either attracted to it or repulsed by it. So strong emotional responses in fact assume the existence of some form of objective reality.

However, if you realize that there is no intrinsic reality to things and events then, of course, this will automatically help you to understand that no matter how real and strong emotions may seem, they have no valid basis. Once you know that they are actually based on a fundamental misconception of reality, then the emotions themselves become untenable. . . .

When you have developed a certain understanding of emptiness, albeit an intellectual one, you will have a new outlook on things and events which you can compare to your usual responses. You will notice how much we tend to project qualities on to the world. More especially, you will realize that most of our strong emotions arise from assuming the reality of something that is unreal. In this way you may be able to gain an experiential sense of the disparity between the way you perceive things and the way things really are.

— *The Four Noble Truths,* 109–10

Mahayana practitioners devote themselves to attaining the state of a Buddha. They work at removing the ignorant, afflictive, selfishly motivated thought patterns that keep them from attaining the fully enlightened, omniscient state that allows them to truly benefit others. Practitioners devote themselves to refining virtuous qualities such as generosity, ethics, and patience to the point where they would give of themselves in any way necessary and would accept all difficulties and injustice in order to serve others. Most important, they develop their wisdom: their realization of emptiness.... Suffice it to say that as one's realization of the emptiness of inherent existence becomes even deeper, all vestiges of selfishness are removed and one approaches the fully enlightened state of Buddhahood. — *An Open Heart,* 164–65

WISDOM AND TRANSFORMATION

According to Buddhism, compassion is an aspiration, a state of mind, wanting others to be free from suffering. It's not passive — it's not empathy alone — but rather an empathetic altruism that actively strives to free others from suffering. Genuine compassion must have both wisdom and loving-kindness. That is to say, one must understand the nature of suffering from which we wish to free others (this is wisdom), and one must experience deep intimacy and empathy with other sentient beings (this is loving-kindness).

The suffering from which we wish to liberate other sentient beings, according to Buddha's teachings, has three levels. The first level includes the obvious physical and mental sensations of pain and discomfort that we all easily identify as suffering. This kind of suffering is primarily at the sensory level — unpleasant or painful sensations and feelings.

The second level of suffering is the suffering of change. Although certain experiences or sensations may seem pleasurable and desirable now, inherent within them is the potential for culminating in an unsatisfactory experience. Another way of saying this is that experiences do not last forever; desirable experiences will eventually be replaced by a neutral experience or an undesirable experience. If it were not the case that desirable experiences are of the nature of change, then, once having a happy experience, we would remain happy forever! In fact, if desirability were intrinsic to an experience, then the longer we remained in contact with it, the happier we would become. However, this is not the case. In fact, often, the more we pursue these experiences, the greater our level of disillusionment, dissatisfaction, and unhappiness becomes.

We can probably find numerous examples of the suffering of change in our lives, but here let us take for example the simple case of someone who buys a new car. For the first few days, the person may be completely happy, utterly pleased with the purchase, constantly thinking about the car, mindfully and lovingly dusting it and cleaning it and polishing it. The person may even feel that he wants to sleep next to it! As time passes, however, the level of excitement and joy is no longer quite as high. Perhaps the person begins to take the car more for granted, or perhaps he begins to regret that he didn't get the more expensive model or different color. Gradually, the level of pleasure from owning the car diminishes, culminating eventually in some form of dissatisfaction — perhaps a desire for another, newer car. That's what we Buddhists mean when we talk about the suffering of change.

The spiritual practitioner needs to cultivate awareness and recognition of this level of suffering. Awareness of this level of suffering is not unique to Buddhists; the aspiration to gain freedom from the suffering of change can be found among non-Buddhist practitioners of meditative absorption.

But the third level of suffering is the most significant — the pervasive suffering of conditioning. This refers to the very fact of our unenlightened existence, the fact that we are ruled by negative emotions and their underlying root cause, namely, our own fundamental ignorance of the nature of reality. Buddhism asserts that as long as we are under control of this fundamental ignorance, we are suffering; this unenlightened existence is suffering by its very nature.

If we are to cultivate the deepest wisdom, we must understand suffering at its deepest, most pervasive level. In turn, freedom from that level of suffering is true nirvana, true liberation, the true state of cessation. . . .

Understanding suffering in this way is the first element of genuine compassion. The second element of genuine compassion, loving-kindness, developing a feeling of intimacy with and empathy toward all beings, must be accomplished on the basis of recognizing our interconnectedness and interdependence with them. We must develop a capacity to connect with others, to feel close to others. This can be accomplished by consciously and intentionally recollecting the limitations and the harmful consequences of self-cherishing — cherishing only one's own well-being — and then reflecting upon the virtues and merits of cherishing the well-being of others. — *Essence of the Heart Sutra*, 49–52

Suffering is a disease we all have. By diagnosing these three types of suffering, we can, over time, get a grasp on the full scope of the disease. — *How to Expand Love*, 89

"Pervasive conditioning" [refers to] the fact that our own mind and body do not operate completely under our own control, but under the influences of karma (tendencies created by previous actions) and emotions such as lust and hatred. In ordinary life we are born from and into the pervasive influence of karma and afflictive emotions. Even when we do not think we are feeling anything, we are under the influence of causes and conditions beyond our control—stuck in a cycle that is prone to suffering. When you realize how this cycle makes you susceptible to all sorts of unwanted events, you want to get rid of it as much as you would want to remove a speck of dust from your eye.

— *How to Expand Love,* 89

"Renunciation" does not refer to the act of giving up all our possessions, but rather to a state of mind. As long as our minds continue to be driven by ignorance, there is no room for lasting happiness, and we remain susceptible to problem after problem. To cut through this cycle, we need to understand the nature of this suffering of conditioned existence and cultivate a strong wish to gain freedom from it. This is true renunciation.

— *Essence of the Heart Sutra,* 38

Nagarjuna [second-century Buddhist philosopher] writes in his Letter to a Friend, "We wish happiness but we chase sorrow. We wish to avoid sorrow but we run directly to it." All beings seek happiness; but most of them, lacking knowledge of how to gain it, find themselves continually immersed in frustration and pain. What we need is an effective approach.

— *The Path to Enlightenment,* 35

The five aggregates are the physical and mental elements that together constitute the existence of an individual. Since the five aggregates are devoid of intrinsic existence (i.e., existing independently or separate from causes and conditions), so too is the individual being constituted by those aggregates. And since the "I," the individual, is devoid of intrinsic existence, devoid of self, so too are all things that are "mine" devoid of intrinsic existence. In other words, not only does the individual — the "appropriator" of physical and mental aggregates — lack intrinsic existence, all the physical and mental aggregates — the appropriated — also lack intrinsic existence. . . .

As we go through this process of negation, it may seem we are in danger of arriving at the specious conclusion that nothing exists. But, if we understand the meaning of emptiness clearly, as I hope we will begin to, we'll see that this is not what is meant. — *Essence of the Heart Sutra,* 84

If one understands the term "soul" as a continuum of individuality from moment to moment, from lifetime to lifetime, then one can say that Buddhism also accepts a concept of soul; there is a kind of continuum of consciousness. From that point of view, the debate on whether or not there is a soul becomes strictly semantic. However, in the Buddhist doctrine of selflessness, or "no soul" theory, the understanding is that there is no eternal, unchanging, abiding, permanent self called "soul." That is what is being denied in Buddhism.

— *Healing Anger,* 30

The world is made up of a network of complex interrelations. We cannot speak of the reality of a discrete entity outside the context of its range of interrelations with its environment and other phenomena, including language, concepts, and other conventions. Thus, there are no subjects without the objects by which they are defined, and there are no objects without subjects to apprehend them, there are no doers without things done. There is no chair

without legs, a seat, a back, wood, nails, the floor on which
it rests, the walls that define the room it's in, the people who
constructed it, and the individuals who agree to call it a chair
and recognize it as something to sit on. Not only is the existence
of things and events utterly contingent, but, according to this
principle, their very identities are thoroughly dependent upon
others.   —*The Universe in a Single Atom*, 64

[In the *Flower Ornament Scripture*] . . . in beautiful poetic verses,
the text compares the intricate and profoundly interconnected
reality of the world to an infinite net of gems called "Indra's
jeweled net," which reaches out to infinite space. At each knot
on the net is a crystal gem, which is connected to all the other
gems and reflects in itself all the others. On such a net, no jewel is
in the center or at the edge. Each and every jewel is at the center
in that it reflects in itself all the others. At the same time, it is at
the edge in that it is itself reflected in all the other jewels. Given
the profound interconnectedness of everything in the universe,
it is not possible to have total knowledge of even a single atom
unless one is omniscient. To know even one atom fully would
imply knowledge of its relations to all other phenomena in the
infinite universe.   —*The Universe in a Single Atom*, 89

The theory of karma is of signal importance in Buddhist thought
but is easily misrepresented. Literally, *karma* means "action"
and refers to the intentional acts of sentient beings. Such acts
may be physical, verbal, or mental — even just thoughts or
feelings — all of which have impacts upon the psyche of an
individual, no matter how minute. Intentions result in acts,
which result in effects that condition the mind toward certain
traits and propensities, all of which give rise to further intentions and actions. The entire process is seen as an endless
self-perpetuating dynamic. The chain reaction of interlocking

causes and effects operates not only in individuals but also for groups and societies, not just in one lifetime but across many lifetimes. — *The Universe in a Single Atom,* 109

There seems to be a consensus among all Buddhist traditions that so far as the actual elimination of the afflictive emotions and cognitive events is concerned, the application of wisdom is necessary; it is indispensable. . . .

Insight into selflessness is seen as the direct antidote to delusions, or afflictive emotions and cognitive events, and insight into the ultimate nature of reality or the ultimate emptiness of phenomena is seen as the direct antidote that would root out the imprints and the residual potencies that are implanted in one's psyche by the delusions. — *Healing Anger,* 47

If you know that someone is speaking badly of you behind your back, and if you react to that negativity with a feeling of hurt or anger, then you yourself destroy your own peace of mind. One's pain is one's own creation. There is a Tibetan expression that one should treat such things as if they were wind behind one's ear. In other words, just brush it aside.

— *Healing Anger,* 55

When someone inflicts harm or injury upon us, if instead of responding positively by developing patience and tolerance we retaliate and take revenge upon him or her, then it will establish a kind of vicious circle. If one retaliates, the other is not going to accept that and he or she is going to retaliate, and then one will do the same, and it will go on. When this happens at the community level, it can go on from generation to generation in a vicious circle. So the result is that both sides suffer. The whole purpose of life is spoiled. For example, in the refugee camps, from childhood hate grows, and some people consider that strong hatred good for the national interest. I think this is very negative, very short-sighted.   *— Healing Anger, 58*

For people who have the problem of self-hatred or self-loathing, for the time being it is advisable that they not think seriously about the suffering nature of existence or the underlying unsatisfactory nature of existence. Rather they should concentrate on the positive aspects of existence, such as appreciating the potentials that lie within oneself as a human being, the opportunities that one's existence as a human being affords. In the traditional teaching, one speaks about all the qualities of a fully endowed human existence. By reflecting upon these opportunities and potentials, one will be able to increase one's sense of worth and confidence.   *— Healing Anger, 66*

How can we eliminate the deepest source of all unsatisfactory experience? Only by cultivating certain qualities in our mindstream. Unless we possess high spiritual qualifications, there is no doubt that the events life throws upon us will give rise to frustration, emotional turmoil, and other distorted states of consciousness. These imperfect states of mind in turn give rise to imperfect activities, and the seeds of suffering are ever planted in steady flow. On the other hand, when the mind can dwell in wisdom that knows the ultimate mode of being, one is able to destroy the deepest root of distortion, negative karma and sorrow.

Our grasping at an inherently existent reality is not something with any strong support. The quality of concreteness, which is our ordinary process of perception we project upon everything, has no actual basis in the objects of our knowledge. The sense of inherent self-being that we feel is there in objects is merely a creation of our own mind, and, if we were to investigate for ourselves, it is unmasked as the source of all our suffering. From this grasping at inherent existence stems the entire range of delusion, emotional afflictions, and their ill-directed activities. Alternatively, by eliminating this method of viewing things, we eliminate the direct source of distorted states of mind as well as the activities they produce.

The force that severs this inborn process of grasping at true existence is the higher training in wisdom. This is the most important method in the quest for eternal liberation. However, to intensify and stabilize the higher training in wisdom, one should also cultivate the higher trainings in meditative concentration and ethical discipline. — *The Path to Enlightenment*, 129–30

SENSIBILITIES AND TRUTHS

You are your own protector; comfort and discomfort are in your hands. — *Advice on Dying*, 61

One of the Tibetan Kadampa masters, Potowa, said that for a meditator who has a certain degree of inner stability and realization, every experience comes as teaching; every event, every experience one is exposed to comes as a kind of learning experience. I think this is very true. — *Healing Anger*, 45

The more honest you are, the more open, the less fear you will have, because there's no anxiety about being exposed or revealed to others. So, I think that the more honest you are, the more self-confident you will be. — *Art of Happiness*, 280

So I think that to a large extent, whether you suffer depends on how you *respond* to a given situation. For example, say that you find out that someone is speaking badly of you behind your back. If you react to this knowledge that someone is speaking badly of you, this negativity, with a feeling of hurt or anger, then *you yourself* destroy your own peace of mind. On the other hand, if you refrain from reacting in a negative way, let the slander pass you by as if it were a silent wind passing behind your ears, you protect yourself from that feeling of hurt, that feeling of agony. So, although you may not be able to avoid difficult situations, you can modify the extent to which you suffer by how you choose to respond to the situation.

— *Art of Happiness*, 152

An open heart is an open mind. A change of heart is a change of mind. — *An Open Heart*, 84

Control over one's future evolution is to be won during one's life, not at the time of death. The yogi Milarepa said, "Fearing death I took to the mountains. Now I have realized the ultimate nature of mind and no longer need to fear." The root cause of one's spiritual development is oneself. Buddha said, "We are our own savior or we are our own enemy." Until now we have lived largely under the power of delusions and, as a result, although we instinctively desire happiness we create only the causes of frustration and sorrow. We wish to avoid suffering, but because our minds are not cultivated in wisdom, we run directly toward suffering like a moth caught in the light of a flame. — *The Path to Enlightenment*, 33

It is the nature of cyclic existence that what has gathered will be dispersed — parents, children, brothers, sisters, and friends. No matter how much friends like each other, eventually they must separate. Gurus and students, parents and children, brothers and sisters, husbands and wives, and friends — no matter who they are — must eventually separate.

While my senior tutor, Ling Rinpochay, was healthy, it was almost impossible, unbearable, for me to think about his death. For me, he was always like a very solid rock on which I could rely. I wondered how I could survive without him. But when he suffered a stroke, after which there was a second, very serious stroke, eventually the situation allowed part of my mind to think, "Now it would be better for him to go." Sometimes I have even thought that he deliberately took on that illness, so that when he did actually pass away, I would be ready to handle the next task — to search for his incarnation.

In addition to separating from all our friends, the wealth and resources that accumulate over time — no matter how marvelous they are — eventually become unusable. No matter how high your rank or position, you must eventually fall. To remind myself of this, when I ascend the high platform from which I teach, just as I am sitting down, I recite to myself the words of the Diamond Cutter Sutra about impermanence:

View things compounded from causes
To be like twinkling stars, figments seen with an eye
    disease,
The flickering light of a butter lamp, magical illusions,
Dew, bubbles, dreams, lightning, and clouds.

I reflect on the fragility of caused phenomena, and then snap my fingers, the brief sound symbolizing impermanence. This is how I remind myself that I will soon be descending from the high throne.   — *Advice on Dying,* 94–95

In the Buddhist text *A Guide to the Bodhisattva Way of Life,* the great scholar Shantideva mentions that it is very important to ensure that a person does not get into a situation which leads to dissatisfaction, because dissatisfaction is the seed of anger. This means that one must adopt a certain outlook toward one's material possessions, toward one's companions and friends, and toward various situations.

Our feelings of dissatisfaction, unhappiness, loss of hope, and so forth are in fact related to all phenomena. If we do not adopt the right outlook, it is possible that anything and everything could cause us frustration. For some people, even the name of the Buddha could conceivably cause anger and frustration, although it may not be the case when someone has a direct personal encounter with a Buddha. Therefore, all phenomena have the potential to create frustration and dissatisfaction in us. Yet phenomena are part of reality and we are subject to the laws of existence. So this leaves us only one option: to change our own attitude. By bringing about a change in our outlook toward things and events, all phenomena can become sources of happiness, instead of sources of frustration.

— Power of Compassion, 52–53

When, at some point in our lives, we meet a real tragedy — which could happen to any one of us — we can react in two ways. Obviously we can lose hope, let ourselves slip into discouragement, into alcohol, drugs, unending sadness. Or else we can wake ourselves up, discover in ourselves an energy that was hidden there, and act with more clarity, more force.

— Violence and Compassion, 140

Spiritual happiness is not like that gained through materialistic, political, or social success, which can be robbed from us by a change in circumstances at any moment and which anyway will definitely be left behind at death. As spiritual happiness does not depend solely upon deceptive conditions such as material supports, a particular environment, or a specific situation, then even if these are withdrawn it has further supports.

— The Path to Enlightenment, 34

2

Morality

The practice of morality is inextricably linked to the process and goal of Buddhist spirituality. The goal of spiritual practice is "attaining" nirvana. While Buddhism offers several classic denotations of the term "nirvana," one of them is indicated by etymology. The word "nirvana" means "to blow out" or "to extinguish." Nirvana, in this case, means the cessation of anger and hatred, craving and greed, and all delusional mental states driven by selfishness or self-centeredness. A Buddha, an enlightened one, cannot but act with wisdom and compassion, and for this reason realizes a unique ontological and moral class, one that is neither "godly" (for gods are impermanent in Buddhism) nor even human, for what typically characterizes human personality are precisely the conflicting psychological impulses. Sometimes we are kind. Sometimes we are selfish. But to "attain" nirvana means that a Buddha spontaneously expresses wisdom and compassion in each and every action. A Buddha, therefore, is unique, a different species, as it were.[1]

As part of the process of the spiritual life, the practice of morality is essential: there can be no wholesome spiritual

---

1. Rupert Gethin, *The Foundations of Buddhism* (Oxford: Oxford University Press, 1990), 29.

*evolution without the active restraint of untoward impulses and
the pro-active cultivation of constructive ones. These steps are
often difficult, owing to strong urges and habits, but their benefits are obvious. On the one hand, our mind becomes more
calm and clear, less buffeted by base instincts. This in turn per-
mits greater freedom and capacity for meditation, which is the
premiere program for spiritual transformation in Buddhism. So
morality issues from metaphysics but segues into meditation.
On the other hand, the fruit of moral lives — lives lived well —
is an anxiety-free life, a life that enjoys measures of peace and
contentment. While this may not be nirvana itself, it is a precondition for nirvana. However, this mental state is also compelling
by itself. We want peace; we want contentment. The Buddhist
emphasis on morality says the way to achieve this is to throttle
back on selfishness and greed and instead cultivate kindness and
generosity. This is happiness.*

*The Dalai Lama is typically encouraging as he promotes
morality, recognizing that moral purification does not happen
rapidly, but incrementally. Indeed, he recounts the story of a
renowned Tibetan hermit who carefully monitored the workings of his mind in his meditation. The monk marked the wall
of his hermitage with a black slash for each unvirtuous thought.
Soon, his entire cell was covered in black. But with mindful
awareness, he gradually cultivated more skillful or wholesome
mental states, and white marks began to replace black ones.
The moral, of course, is that integrating wisdom and compassion occurs little by little. Indeed, the call to patience and
self-compassion in the path of holiness is hardly limited to Buddhism, but Buddhism certainly emphasizes the importance of a
gradual process in moral and spiritual evolution.*[2]

2. See my own cross-cultural exploration of holiness and human flourishing,
Soulsong: Seeking Holiness, Coming Home (Maryknoll, N.Y.: Orbis Books, 2006).

PREMISES

What do people understand a good life to be? It cannot be equated with a pleasant life in which all our material wishes and dreams are fulfilled. Instead it is a life lived in ethical responsibility. A life in which we do not think only of our own well-being but also serve others.

— Path of Wisdom, Path of Peace, 61

Kindness is essential to mental peace. *— How to Practice,* 95

Compassion also brings us an inner strength. Once it is developed, it naturally opens an inner door, through which we can communicate with fellow human beings, and even other sentient beings, with ease, and heart to heart.

— The Four Noble Truths, 136

What is the main thrust of Buddhist practices concerning behavior? It is to tame one's mental continuum — to become nonviolent. *— The Meaning of Life,* 4

I like to say that the essence of the Buddha's teaching can be found in two sayings:

If possible, you should help others.
If that is not possible, at least you should do no harm.

Refraining from harming others is the essence of the initial stage of living the teachings of morality.

— How to Practice, 70–71

It is important to understand that counterproductive actions of body and speech do not just arise by themselves, but spring from a dependence upon mental motivation. The influence of faulty states of mind causes faulty actions to be produced. Thus, to control negative physical and verbal actions, it is necessary to get at their root, the mind, and tame it. This level of the practice of love can be included within one sentence: "Do not harm others."   — *How to Expand Love*, 81

Imagine a situation where we inconvenience another in some small way, perhaps by bumping into them accidentally while walking along, and they shout at us for being careless. We are much more likely to shrug this off if our disposition (*kun long*) is wholesome, if our hearts are suffused with compassion, than if we are under the sway of negative emotions. When the driving force of our actions is wholesome, our actions will tend automatically to contribute to others' well-being. They will thus automatically be ethical. Further, the more this is our habitual state, the less likely we are to react badly when provoked. And even when we do lose our temper, any outburst will be free of any sense of malice or hatred. In my view, then, the aim of spiritual and, therefore, ethical practice is to transform and perfect the individual's *kun long*. This is how we become better human beings.   — *Ethics for a New Millennium*, 32

COMPASSION

For our religion, *mahakaruna*, the great healing kindness toward all sentient beings, is the most important thing.
                              — *Path of Wisdom, Path of Peace*, 52

Kindness is essential to mental peace.   — *How to Practice*, 5

Compassion also brings us an inner strength. Once it is developed, it naturally opens an inner door, through which we can communicate with fellow human beings, and even other sentient beings, with ease, and heart to heart.

—*The Four Noble Truths*, 136

Genuine love does not depend on a special relationship. It does not need a personal bond. This is why we must learn not to confuse feelings of affection or falling in love with true love. All too often, friendliness toward our fellow humans disappears when personal affection disappears. In that case, we are nice to someone only as long as we like that person.

Mahakaruna, great loving-kindness toward all beings, is the basic attitude of Mahayana Buddhism. For us it is the most precious thing. We say that it will exist as long as there are suffering beings. We can let our compassion become greater and greater because there are no boundaries to loving-kindness.

—*Path of Wisdom, Path of Peace*, 58

Compassion is of little value if it remains an idea. It must become our attitude toward others, reflected in all our thoughts and actions. And the mere concept of humility does not diminish our arrogance; it must become our actual state of being.

—*An Open Heart*, 48

Genuine compassion must be unconditional.

—*An Open Heart*, 110

What, then, is the relationship between spirituality and ethical practice? Since love and compassion and similar qualities all, by definition, presume some level of concern for others' well-being, they presume ethical restraint. We cannot be loving and compassionate unless at the same time we curb our own harmful impulses and desires.   —*Ethics for a New Millennium*, 26

If one examines [a morally problematic] situation carefully, one will see that many harmful acts are caused not out of malicious intention, but out of carelessness or a lack of sensitivity.

— Healing Anger, 52

Our normal state of mind is heavily biased. We have an attitude of distance from people that we consider as unfriendly or enemies and a disproportionate sense of closeness or attachment toward those whom we consider to be our friends. We can see how our emotional response toward others is fluctuating and biased. Until we overcome these prejudices, we have no possibility of generating genuine compassion. Even though we might be able to feel a certain amount of compassion toward some people, that compassion, as long as it is not based on profound equanimity, will remain biased, for it is mixed with attachment.

If you look at compassion mixed with attachment, no matter how intense and strong that mixed emotion may be, you will realize that it is based on your projection of certain positive qualities onto the object of your compassion — whether the object is a close friend, a family member, or whomever. Depending on your changing attitudes toward that object, your emotional feelings will also change. For example, in a relationship with a friend, suddenly one day you may no longer be able to see in that person the good qualities that you had previously perceived, and this new attitude would immediately affect your feelings toward that person. Genuine compassion, on the other hand, springs from a clear recognition of the experience of suffering on the part of the object of compassion, and from the realization that this creature is worthy of compassion and affection. Any compassionate feeling that arises from these two realizations cannot be swayed — no matter how that object of compassion reacts against you. Even if the object reacts in a very negative way, this won't have the power to influence your compassion. Your compassion will remain the same or become even more powerful.

If you carefully examine the nature of compassion, you will also find that genuine compassion can be extended even to one's enemies, those whom you consider hostile toward you. In contrast, compassion mixed with attachment cannot be extended to someone whom you consider to be your enemy. Conventionally speaking, we define an enemy as someone who either directly harms us or hurts us, or someone who is motivated to or has the intention to harm or hurt us. The realization that such a person is fully intent on hurting and harming you cannot give rise to the feeling of closeness and empathy as long as such feelings require an attachment to the person. However, this realization that another person wishes to harm and hurt you cannot undermine genuine compassion — a compassion based on the clear recognition of that person as someone who is suffering, someone who has the natural and instinctual desire to seek happiness and overcome suffering, just as oneself. In the Christian spiritual context, this could be extended by thinking along the following lines: just as myself, this enemy shares the same divine nature and is a creation of the divine force. So on these grounds, that person is worthy of my compassion and a feeling of closeness toward him or her. This kind of compassion or feeling of empathy is genuine compassion free of attachment.
— *The Good Heart*, 68–69

Compassion diminishes fright about your own pain and increases inner strength. — *Advice on Dying*, 53

In order to transform ourselves — our habits and dispositions — so that our actions are compassionate, it is necessary to develop what we might call an *ethic of virtue*. As well as refraining from negative thoughts and emotions, we need to cultivate and reinforce our positive qualities. What are these positive qualities? Our basic human, or spiritual qualities.

After compassion (*nying je*) itself, the chief of these is what in Tibetan we call *sö pa*. Once again, we have a term which appears to have no ready equivalent in other languages, though the ideas it conveys are universal. Often, *sö pa* is translated simply as "patience," though its literal meaning is "able to bear" or "able to withstand." But the word also carries a notion of resolution. It thus denotes a deliberate response (as opposed to an unreasoned reaction) to the strong negative thoughts and emotions that tend to arise when we encounter harm. As such, *sö pa* is what provides us with the strength to resist suffering and protects us from losing compassion even for those who would harm us.

In this context, I am reminded of the example of Lopon-la, a monk from Namgyal, the Dalai Lama's own monastery. Following my escape from Tibet, Lopon-la was one of many thousands of monks and officials imprisoned by the occupying forces. When he was finally released, he was allowed to come to India, where he rejoined his old monastery. More than twenty years after last seeing him, I found Lopon-la much as I remembered him. He looked older, of course, but physically he was unscathed, and mentally his ordeal had not affected him adversely at all. His gentleness and serenity remained. From our conversation, I learned that he had, nevertheless, endured grievous treatment during those long years of imprisonment. In common with all others, he had been subjected to "re-education," during which he had been forced to denounce his religion, and, on many occasions, he was tortured as well. When I asked him whether he had ever been afraid, he admitted that there was one thing that had scared him: the possibility that he might lose compassion and concern for his jailers.

—*Ethics for the New Millennium,* 102

Within all beings there is the seed of perfection. However, compassion is required to activate that seed which is inherent in our hearts and minds. — *The Art of Happiness, 71–72*

A disciplined attitude of true other-concern, in which you cherish others more than yourself, is helpful both to you and to others. It does no harm to anyone, temporarily or in the long run. Compassion is a priceless jewel. — *How to Practice, 93*

Put others first; you yourself come next. This works even from a selfish viewpoint. Let me explain how this is possible. You want happiness and do not want suffering, and if you show other people kindness, love, and respect, they will respond in kind; this way your happiness will increase. If you show other people anger and hatred, they will show you the same, and you will lose your own happiness. So I say, if you are selfish, you should be *wisely* selfish. Ordinary selfishness focuses only on your own needs, but if you are wisely selfish, you will treat others just as you treat those close to you. Ultimately, this strategy will produce more satisfaction, more happiness. So even from a selfish viewpoint, you get better results by respecting others, serving others, and reducing self-centeredness. — *How to Practice, 81*

A loving altruistic attitude has only one face, kindness to others. — *How to Expand Love, 76*

Genuine peace of mind is rooted in affection and compassion. There is a very high level of sensitivity and feeling involved. So long as we lack an inner discipline, an inner calmness of mind, then no matter what external facilities or conditions we may have, they will never give us the feeling of joy and happiness that we seek. On the other hand, if we possess this inner quality, that is, calmness of mind, a degree of stability within, then even if we lack the various external facilities that are normally considered necessary for a happy and joyful life, it is still possible to live a happy and joyful life.   —*Healing Anger,* 9

There is no secret method by which compassion and loving-kindness can come about. We must knead our minds skillfully, and with patience and perseverance we shall find that our concern for the well-being of others will grow.

—*An Open Heart,* 106

Once you accept the fact that compassion is not something childish or sentimental, once you realize that compassion is something really worthwhile, realize its deeper value, then you immediately develop an attraction toward it, a willingness to cultivate it.

And once you encourage the thought of compassion in your mind, once that thought becomes active, then your attitude toward others changes automatically. If you approach others with the thought of compassion, that will automatically reduce fear and allow an openness with other people. It creates a positive, friendly atmosphere....

I think that in many cases people tend to expect the other person to respond to them in a positive way first, rather than taking the initiative themselves to create that possibility. I feel that's wrong; it leads to problems and can act as a barrier that just serves to promote a feeling of isolation from others. So, if you wish to overcome that feeling of isolation and loneliness, I think that your underlying attitude makes a tremendous difference. And approaching others with the thought of compassion in your mind is the best way to do this.

—*The Art of Happiness,* 69–70

THE ENEMY

When we are faced with an enemy, a person or group of people wishing us harm, we can view this as an opportunity to develop patience and tolerance. We need these qualities; they are useful to us. And the only occasion we have to develop them is when we are challenged by an enemy. So, from this point of view, our enemy is our guru, our teacher. Irrespective of motivation, from our point of view enemies are very beneficial, a blessing.

— *An Open Heart*, 21

The enemy is the greatest teacher for our practice. Shantideva argues very brilliantly that enemies, or the perpetrators of harm upon us, are in fact objects worthy of respect and are worthy of being regarded as our precious teachers. . . . It is his or her very intention of harming us which makes that person an enemy and because of that the enemy provides us with an opportunity to practice tolerance and patience. Therefore the enemy is indeed a precious teacher. — *The Power of Compassion*, 54–55

I consider hatred to be the ultimate enemy. By "enemy" I mean the person or factor which directly or indirectly destroys our interest. Our interest is that which ultimately creates happiness.

We can also speak of the external enemy. For example, in my own case, our Chinese brothers and sisters are destroying Tibetan rights and, in that way, more suffering and anxiety develops. But no matter how forceful this is, it cannot destroy the supreme source of my happiness, which is calmness of mind. This is something an external enemy cannot destroy. Our country can be invaded, our possessions can be destroyed, our friends can be killed, but these are secondary for our mental happiness. The ultimate source of my mental happiness is my peace of mind. Nothing can destroy this except my own anger.

— *The Power of Compassion*, 50

When friends are overemphasized, enemies also come to be overemphasized. When you are born, you do not know anyone and no one knows you. Even though all of us equally want happiness and do not want suffering, you like the faces of some people and think, "These are *my* friends," and dislike the faces of others and think, "These are *my* enemies." You affix identities and nicknames to them and end up practicing the generation of desire for the former and the generation of hatred for the latter. What value is there in this? None. The problem is that so much energy is being expended on concern for a level no deeper than the superficial affairs of this life. The profound loses out to the trivial.   — *Advice on Dying,* 50–51

If someone treats us unjustly, we must first analyze the situation. If we feel we can bear the injustice, if the negative consequences of doing so are not too great, then I think it best to accept it. However, if in our judgment, reached with clarity and awareness, we are led to the conclusion that acceptance would bring greater negative consequences, then we must take appropriate countermeasures. This conclusion should be reached on the basis of clear awareness of the situation and not as a result of anger. I think that anger and hatred actually cause more harm to us than to the person responsible for our problem.

                                                           — *An Open Heart,* 20

ANGER AND AFFLICTIVE EMOTION

Through anger we lose one of the best human qualities — the power of judgment.   — *A Policy of Kindness,* 50

The main cure is to realize how harmful, how negative, anger is. Once you realize very, very convincingly how negative it is, that realization itself has power to reduce anger. You must see that it always brings unhappiness and trouble.

Of course anger comes. Anger is like a friend or relative which you cannot avoid and always have to associate with. When you get to know him you realize that he is difficult and you have to be careful. Every time you meet that person — still on friendly terms — you take some precaution. As a result the influence that he has over you grows less and less. In the same way you see the anger coming, but you realize "Ah, it always brings trouble, there is not much point to it." The anger will lose its power or force. So with time it gets weaker and weaker.

— *A Policy of Kindness*, 93

If we examine how anger or hateful thoughts arise in us, we will find that, generally speaking, they arise when we feel hurt, when we feel that we have been unfairly treated by someone against our expectations. If in that instant we examine carefully the way anger arises, there is a sense that it comes as a protector, comes as a friend that would help our battle or in taking revenge against the person who has inflicted harm on us. So the anger or hateful thought that arises appears to come as a shield or a protector. But in reality, that is an illusion. It is a very delusory state of mind.

— *Healing Anger*, 9

Afflictive emotions deceive us. They seem to offer satisfaction. But they do not provide it. In fact, although such emotion comes to us in the guise of a protector, as it were, giving us boldness and strength, we find that this energy is essentially blind. Decisions taken under its influence are often a source of regret. More often than not, such anger is actually an indication of weakness rather than of strength. Most people have experienced an argument deteriorating to the point where one person becomes verbally abusive, a clear sign of the fragility of their position. Moreover, we do not need anger to develop courage and confidence. As we shall see, it can be done through other means.

The afflictive emotions also have an irrational dimension. They encourage us to suppose that appearances are invariably commensurate with reality. When we become angry or feel hatred, we tend to relate to others as if their characteristics were immutable. A person can appear to be objectionable from the crown of their head to the soles of their feet. We forget that they, like us, are merely suffering human beings with the same wish to be happy and to avoid suffering as we ourselves. Yet common sense alone tells us that when the force of our anger diminishes, they are sure to seem a little better at least. The same is true in reverse when individuals become infatuated. The other appears to be wholly desirable — until such time as the grip of afflictive emotion subsides and they come to seem a little less than perfect. Indeed, when our passions become so strongly aroused, there is considerable danger of going to the opposite extreme. The individual once idolized now seems despicable and hateful, though of course it is the same person throughout.

The afflictive emotions are also useless. The more we give in to them, the less room we have for our good qualities — for kindness and compassion — and the less able we are to solve our problems. Indeed, there is no occasion when these disturbing thoughts and emotions are helpful either to ourselves or to others....

Nowhere is the uselessness of afflictive emotion more obvious than in the case of anger. When we become angry, we stop being compassionate, loving, generous, forgiving, tolerant, and patient altogether. We thus deprive ourselves of the very things that happiness consists in. And not only does anger immediately destroy our critical faculties, it tends toward rage, spite, hatred, and malice — each of which is always negative because it is a direct cause of harm for others. Anger causes suffering....

I do not deny that, as in the case of fear, there is a kind of "raw" anger that we experience more as a rush of energy than as a cognitively enhanced emotion. Conceivably, this form of anger could have positive consequences. It is not impossible to imagine anger at the sight of injustice which causes someone to act altruistically. The anger that causes us to go to the assistance of someone who is being attacked in the street could be characterized as positive. But if this goes beyond meeting the injustice, if it becomes personal and turns into vengefulness or maliciousness, then danger arises. When we do something negative, we are capable of recognizing the difference between ourselves and the negative act. But we often fail to separate action and agent when it comes to others. This shows us how unreliable is even apparently justified anger.

Should it still seem too much to say that anger is an entirely useless emotion, we can ask ourselves if anyone ever says anger can bring happiness. No one does. What doctor prescribes anger as a treatment for any disease? There isn't one. Anger can only hurt us. It has nothing to recommend it. Let the reader ask himself or herself: When we become angry, do we feel happy? Does our mind become calmer and our body relax? Or rather is it not that we feel tense in body and unsettled of mind?

If we are to retrain our peace of mind and thereby our happiness, it follows that alongside a more rational and disinterested approach to our negative thoughts and emotions, we must cultivate a strong habit of restraint in response to them.

— *Ethics for the New Millennium*, 93–97

The negative emotions such as hatred, anger, and desire are our real enemies which disturb and destroy our mental happiness and cause disturbance in society. Therefore, they are to be totally abandoned; they do not have even the slightest potential for yielding happiness.   —*A Policy of Kindness*, 96

The heart of renunciation is a quest for a victory over the internal enemy, the mental afflictions.
                                   —*Essence of the Heart Sutra*, 38

Anger cannot be overcome by anger. If a person shows anger to you, and you respond with anger, the result is disastrous. In contrast, if you control anger and show opposite attitudes — compassion, tolerance, and patience — then not only do you yourself remain in peace, but the other's anger will gradually diminish.   —*A Policy of Kindness*, 41

[On the limitations of sensory gratifications] This is not to say that the pleasure we take in certain activities is somehow mistaken. But we must acknowledge that there can be no hope of gratifying the senses permanently. At best, the happiness we derive from eating a good meal can only last until the next time we are hungry. As one ancient Indian writer remarked: Indulging our senses and drinking salt water are alike: the more we partake, the more our desire and thirst grow.
                                   —*Ethics for the New Millennium*, 52

Greed is a form of desire. However, it is an exaggerated form of desire, based on overexpectation.
    The true antidote of greed is contentment.
                                   —*Healing Anger*, 32

Much of Buddhist literature is devoted to exposing the nature of afflictions and the need to overcome them. . . . An affliction, by its very nature, brings about an immediate disturbance within the mind of the individual the moment it arises and thereby causes suffering within that individual.

When we speak in general of our aspiration to be happy and to be free of suffering, we are of course talking about our conscious experiences — that is, our wish to *experience* happiness and not to *experience* suffering....

However, experiences of unhappiness and happiness at the level of *mental* consciousness are far more acute (than purely physical events). If we look carefully, we see that much of our unhappiness and suffering is caused by disturbances in our thoughts and emotions. These are the results of the mental afflictions, the kleshas. Examples of these afflictions include attachment or greed, aversion or hatred, anger, pride, jealousy — the whole range of negative states a human being can experience. All these afflictions, as soon as they arise, immediately disturb our hearts and minds....

In truth, it is always and only the mental afflictions that agitate our minds, yet we tend to blame our agitation on external conditions, imagining that encountering unpleasant people or adverse circumstances makes us unhappy. However, as the great Indian Buddhist teacher Shantideva pointed out around the eighth century, when true practitioners of the Buddha's teachings encounter adversities, they remain resolute and unmoved, like a tree. Shantideva reminds us that encountering adversity, in itself, does not necessarily lead to a disturbed mind; even amid adversity, the principal cause of our unhappiness is our own undisciplined mind under the influence of the kleshas. Failing to understand this principle, we allow ourselves to be controlled by the mental afflictions; in fact, we often embrace and reinforce them, for instance by adding fuel to our anger.

—*Essence of the Heart Sutra*, 31–32

PERSPECTIVES

In general, the difficult periods of life provide the best opportunities to gain useful experiences and develop inner strength.

—*An Open Heart*, 22

Once you know things are always changing, even if you are passing through a very difficult period, you can find comfort in knowing that the situation will not remain that way forever. So, there is no need for frustration.   —*Advice on Dying*, 43

Nonviolence does not mean that we remain indifferent to a problem. On the contrary, it is important to be fully engaged. However, we must behave in a way that does not benefit us alone. We must not harm the interests of others. Nonviolence therefore is not merely the absence of violence. It involves a sense of compassion and caring. It is almost a manifestation of compassion. I strongly believe that we must promote such a concept of nonviolence at the level of the family as well as at the national and international levels. Each individual has the ability to contribute to such compassionate nonviolence.

How should we go about this? We can start with ourselves. We must try to develop greater perspective, looking at situations from all angles. Usually when we face problems, we look at them from our own point of view. We even sometimes deliberately ignore other aspects of a situation. This often leads to negative consequences. However, it is very important for us to have a broader perspective.

We must come to realize that others are also part of our society. We can think of our society as a body, with arms and legs as part of it. Of course, the arm is different from the leg; however, if something happens to the foot, the hand should reach down to help. Similarly, when something is wrong within our society, we must help. Why? Because it is part of the body, it is part of us....

Developing a broader view of our situation and expanding our awareness in themselves can bring about a change in our homes. Sometimes, due to a very small matter, a fight starts between a husband and wife, or between a parent and child. If you look at only one aspect of the situation, focusing merely on the immediate problem, then, yes, it is really worth fighting and quarreling. It is even worth divorcing! However, looking at the situation with more perspective, we see that though there is a problem, there is also a common interest. You can come to think, "This is a small problem that I must solve by dialogue, not by drastic measures." We can thereby develop a nonviolent atmosphere within our own family as well as within our community.　　　　　　　　— *An Open Heart*, 11–13

As the great Indian scholar Shantideva has said, "If there is a way to overcome suffering, then there is no need to worry; if there is no way to overcome the suffering, then there is no use in worrying." That kind of attitude is quite useful.
　　　　　　　　　　　　　— *The Power of Compassion*, 22

It is not enough to make noisy calls to halt moral degeneration; we must do something about it.　　— *How to See Yourself*, 21

Sexual relations are part of nature and without them there would be no more human beings — that is clear.... One must not have just the desire for sexual pleasure, but also a sense of responsibility....

Sometimes people ask me about marriage. Of course I have no experience of it, but I am quite sure about one thing: marriage with too much haste is dangerous. First you must have a long period to examine one another, and afterward, when you have genuine confidence that you can live together, then you should marry.   — *The Power of Compassion*, 15–16

Therefore each of you should feel that you have great potential and that, with self-confidence and a little more effort, change really is possible if you want it.

— *The Power of Compassion*, 49

One renowned Tibetan hermit limited his practice to watching his mind. He drew a black mark on the wall of his room whenever he had an unvirtuous thought. Initially his walls were all black; however, as he became more mindful, his thoughts became more virtuous and white marks began to replace the black ones. We must apply similar mindfulness in our daily lives.

— *An Open Heart*, 62

Ironically, the most serious problems emanate from industrially advanced societies, where unprecedented literacy seems only to have fostered restlessness and discontent.

— *How to See Yourself*, 1

One way to work with deep fears is to think that the fear comes as a result of your own actions in the past. Further, if you have fear of some pain or suffering, you should examine whether there is anything you can do about it. If you can there is no need to worry about it; if you cannot do anything, then there is also no need to worry.

Another technique is to investigate who is becoming afraid. Examine the nature of your self. Where is this I? Who is this I? What is the nature of I? Is there an I besides my physical body and my consciousness? This may help.

Also, someone who is engaging in the Bodhisattva practices seeks to take others' suffering onto himself or herself. When you have fear, you can think, "Others have fear similar to this; may I take to myself all of their fears." Even though you are opening yourself to greater suffering, taking greater suffering to yourself, your fear lessens.

Yet another way is not to let your mind stay with the thought of fear but to put it on something else and let the fear just become lost. That is just a temporary method. Also, if you have a sense of fear due to insecurity, you can imagine for instance, if you are lying down, that your head is in the Buddha's lap. Sometimes this may help psychologically. Another method is to recite mantras. — *A Policy of Kindness, 98–99*

Sincere motivation acts as an antidote to reduce fear and anxiety. — *The Art of Happiness, 270*

If you cultivate a compassionate motivation, if you fail, then there's no regret.

So, again and again, I think that proper motivation can be a sort of protector, shielding you against these feelings of fear and anxiety. Motivation is so important. In fact all human action can be seen in terms of movement, and the mover behind all actions is one's motivation. If you develop a pure and sincere motivation, if you are motivated by a wish to help on the basis of kindness, compassion, and respect, then you can carry on any kind of work, in any field, and function more effectively with less fear of worry, not being afraid of what others think or whether you ultimately will be successful in reaching your goal. Even if you fail to achieve your goal, you can feel good about having made the effort. But with a bad motivation, people can praise you or you can achieve your goals, but you still will not be happy. — *The Art of Happiness, 272*

Discipline does not mean prohibition; rather, it means that when there is a contradiction between long-term and short-term interests, you sacrifice the short-term for the sake of the long-term benefit.   —*Advice on Dying*, 43

To be aware of a single shortcoming within oneself is more useful than to be aware of a thousand in someone else. Rather than speaking badly about people and in ways that will produce friction and unrest in their lives, we should practice a purer perception of them, and when we speak of others, speak of their good qualities. If you find yourself slandering anybody, just fill your mouth with excrement. That will break you of the habit quick enough.   —*A Policy of Kindness*, 96

Human history is in a way a history of human mental thought. Historical events, wars, good developments, tragedies . . . all these are records of negative and positive human thought. All the great persons, the liberators, the great thinkers, all these great human beings of the past, have been produced through positive thought. Tragedy, tyranny, all the terrible wars, all those negative things have happened because of negative human thought. In the human mind both positive and negative thoughts are potentially present. Therefore, the only worthwhile thing for a human being to do is to try to develop the positive thought, to increase its power of force and to reduce the negative thinking. If you do that, human love, forgiveness, kindness will give you more hope and determination. And hope and determination will bring you a brighter future. If you give way to anger, hatred, you get lost. No sensible human being wants to lose himself.   —*A Policy of Kindness*, 94

Look at all the terrible weapons there are. Yet the weapons themselves cannot start a war. The button to trigger them is under a human finger, which moves by thought, not under its own power. The responsibility rests in our thought.

If you look deeply into such things, the blueprint is found within — in the mind — out of which actions come. Thus, first controlling the mind is very important. I am not talking here about controlling the mind in the sense of deep meditation, but just about cultivating less anger, more respect for others' rights, more concern for other people, more clear realization of our sameness as human beings. — *A Policy of Kindness, 49*

I think that if one's life is simple, contentment has to come. Simplicity is extremely important for happiness.

— *A Policy of Kindness, 42*

The sangha, or virtuous community, are those who, practicing the doctrine properly, assist others to gain refuge. They have four special qualities. The first is that if someone harms them, they do not respond with harm; the second is that if someone displays anger to them, they do not react with anger; the third is that if someone insults them, they do not answer with insult; and the fourth is that if someone accuses them, they do not retaliate. This is the style of behavior of a monk or nun. The root of these again meets back to compassion; thus, the main qualities of the spiritual community also stem from compassion. In this way, the three refuges for a Buddhist — Buddha, doctrine, and spiritual community — all have their root in compassion.

— *The Meaning of Life, 5*

By becoming truly aware of others and developing respect for them, we ourselves become much happier and more satisfied, which itself has the outward effect of creating an atmosphere of peace. For example, if in a room full of people someone becomes angry and begins shouting, the atmosphere becomes tense for everyone. However, if every person in a group feels and demonstrates warm feelings and respect for one another, the atmosphere is peaceful and harmonious. The external emanates from the internal.   *— How to Expand Love, 76–77*

That people in need are ignored or abandoned for political reasons reveals what we are lacking — though we are intelligent and powerful, strong enough to exploit peoples and destroy the world, we lack real kindness and love. There is an Indian saying, "When an arrow has hit, there is no time to ask who shot it, or what kind of arrow it was." Similarly, when we encounter human suffering, it is important to respond with commiseration rather than to question the politics of those we help. Instead of asking whether their country is enemy or friend, we must think, These are human beings; they are suffering, and they have a right to happiness equal to our own.

— How to Expand Love, 78

Without the appreciation of kindness, society breaks down. Human society exists because it is impossible to live in complete isolation. We are interdependent by nature, and since we must live together, we should do so with a positive attitude of concern for one another. The aim of human society must be the compassionate betterment of all from one lifetime to the next.

As small children we very much depend on the kindness of our parents. Again in old age we depend on the kindness of others. Between childhood and old age we falsely believe we are independent, but this is not so.

— How to Expand Love, 69–70

Cultivating virtue should not be seen as separate from restraining our response to afflictive emotion. They go hand in hand.

This is why ethical discipline cannot be confined either to mere restraint or to mere affirmation of positive qualities.

To see how the process of restraint coupled with counter-action works, let us consider anxiety. We can describe this as a form of fear, but one with a well-developed mental component. Now we are bound to encounter experiences and events we feel concerned about. But what turns concern into anxiety is when we start to brood and let the imagination add negative reflections. Then we begin to feel anxious and start to worry. And the more we indulge in worry, the more reasons we find for it. Eventually we find ourselves in a state of permanent distress. The more developed this state, the less we are able to take action against it, and the stronger it becomes. But when we think carefully, we see that underlying this process is principally narrowness of vision and a lack of proper perspective. This causes us to ignore the fact that things and events come into being as the result of innumerable causes and conditions. We tend to concentrate on just one or two aspects of our situation. In so doing, we inevitably restrict ourselves to finding means to overcoming only these aspects. The trouble with this is that if we are unable to do so, there is a danger of becoming totally demoralized. The first step in overcoming anxiety is thus to develop a proper perspective of our situation.

This we can do in a number of different ways. One of the most effective is to try to shift the focus of attention away from self and toward others. When we succeed in this, we find that the scale of our own problems diminishes. This is not to say we should ignore our own needs altogether, but rather that we should try to remember others' needs alongside our own, no matter how pressing ours may be. This is helpful, because when our concern for others is translated into action, we find that confidence arises automatically and worry and anxiety diminish. Indeed, we find that almost all the mental and emotional suffering which is such a feature of modern living — including the sense of hopelessness, of loneliness, and so on — lessens the moment we begin to engage in actions motivated by concern for others.   — *Ethics for the New Millennium*, 110–11

The undisciplined mind is like an elephant. If left to blunder around out of control, it will wreak havoc. But the harm and suffering we encounter as a result of failing to restrain the negative impulses of mind far exceed the damage a rampaging elephant can cause.   — *Ethics for the New Millennium*, 82

I should mention that when we speak of a calm state of mind or peace of mind, we shouldn't confuse that with a totally insensitive, apathetic state of mind. Having a calm or peaceful state of mind doesn't mean being totally spaced out or completely empty. Peace of mind or a calm state of mind is rooted in affection and compassion. There is a very high level of sensitivity and feeling there.   — *The Art of Happiness*, 26

The demarcation between a positive and a negative desire or action is not whether it gives you an immediate feeling of satisfaction but whether it ultimately results in positive or negative consequences.   — *The Art of Happiness*, 28

The best relationships are those in which your love for the other is greater than your need for the other.   — Source Unknown

There is no benefit in worrying whatsoever.
                                         — *A Policy of Kindness*, 40

Even if you cannot actually implement the practices of love and compassion, merely hearing about them establishes powerful predispositions for future success. This can be amplified by planting prayer-wishes aspiring to altruism. Do not be discouraged; it is difficult to absorb such a profound perspective. It is particularly important to do the best you can.

—*How to Expand Love,* 83

Usually my advice for beginners is to be patient: have fewer expectations of yourself. It is most important to be an honest citizen, a good member of the human community. Whether or not you understand profound ideas, it is important to be a good person wherever you are right now.   —*How to Practice,* 70

3

Meditation

Although Buddhism weaves an intimate connection between wisdom, morality, and meditation, meditation, arguably, is the pinnacle of Buddhist practice. Philosophy offers a comprehensive understanding of the nature of reality and, therefore, offers a justification for meditative experience. The intentional effort involved in meditative practice implies the process of internalizing wisdom. In meditation, theory meets practice; intellectual knowledge becomes knowledge by acquaintance. Meditation deepens and intensifies the work of morality by purifying the mind of the distortions owing to chronic self-centeredness. In a sense, the meditation rewires the circuitry of our perceiving. By generating a psychic distance from our biological, emotional, psychological, and social conditioning, meditation creates a space that allows freedom from our usual reactive patterns. These, when deepened by repeated and longstanding habits, create a kind of automatic default; in a sense, we lose our freedom, our autonomy. We are no longer lords of ourselves. There are many kinds of meditation, but we might say a cardinal goal is to see things as they are, free of the distortions of selfishness. In this case, proper meditation is both cognitive and emotional therapy. When we see things rightly, we will no longer be under

the sway of emotional reactivity. Instead, we will see the intimate interconnections between all phenomenal events, and this leads to compassion. To put it another way, wisdom recognizes that suffering anywhere is our suffering. Compassion naturally moves to mitigate it. Compassion, then, is a logical outcome of seeing the reality as it is, namely, as inter-connected, inter-related, and inter-dependent.

The Dalai Lama has written much and lucidly on meditation. Some forms of meditation are rather analytical, breaking things down, bearing rational examination upon phenomenal events, deconstructing or dissolving, above all, the concept of self. One of the great hobbies of the Dalai Lama perfectly reflects this approach. He repairs watches. With eyeglass and tools at hand, he enjoys breaking the watch down into its component parts, observing the interconnections, facilitating, by careful adjustments, new and improved functioning. This is a decidedly pragmatic and empirical approach. And it carries over to meditation. Meditation brings awareness of the component elements of our personhood, scrutinizes their workings and interactions, and aims to facilitate healthy mental functioning. Meditation facilitates a fluid movement of our internal world, and, consequently, in our experience of the external world.

The Dalai Lama has often called himself a simple monk. One of his deepest desires, expressed so effectively in the documentary Compassion in Exile, *is to withdraw from the public stage at some point in order to cultivate more intensely his meditative practice. Knowing that so much of religious practice is preparation for death, he has also expressed, with typical inquisitiveness, a desire to see at the end of his life the outcome of all such practice. Again, with an attitude that is disarming and unpretentious, the Dalai Lama reveals a humble curiosity to learn, in the end, the ultimate effectiveness of such preparation.*

PREMISES

Even for a nonbeliever, just a simple honest human being, the ultimate source of happiness is in our mental attitude. Even if you have good health, material facilities used in the proper way and good relations with other human beings, the main cause of a happy life is within.   — *The Power of Compassion*, 49

Our meditation can be compatible with every type of belief. As I would like to say to people everywhere on the earth time and again, world peace begins in a peaceful heart. This is nothing other than letting love and compassion grow in our own hearts, overcoming the inner unrest that plagues us all.
                                         — *Path of Wisdom, Path of Peace*, 88

Even from the point of view of your personal well-being, you must cultivate a compassionate mind — that is the source of happiness in your life.   — *Stages of Meditation*, 72

Compassion is the very essence of an open heart and must be cultivated throughout our journey. Equanimity removes our prejudices and enables our altruism to reach all sentient beings. *Bodhicitta* is the commitment to actually help them.
                                         — *An Open Heart*, 125

Though virtuous and nonvirtuous actions are performed by body, speech, and mind, the mind is most important, so the root of Buddhist practice is transformation of the mind. The emphasis of Buddhist teaching is on a tamed mind — the foundation of which is the perception that you are the creator of your own pleasure and pain.   — *Advice on Dying*, 60

Training the mind is a process of familiarization. In the Buddhist context, familiarization, or meditation, refers to the positive transformation of the mind, that is, to the elimination of its defective qualities and the improvement of its positive qualities. Through meditation we can train our minds in such a way that negative qualities are abandoned and positive qualities are generated and enhanced. — *Meditation*, 36

The principal tool for purifying the mind is the mind itself.
— *Violence and Compassion*, 136

Although we all naturally aspire to be happy and wish to overcome our misery, we continue to experience pain and suffering. Why is this? Buddhism teaches that we actually conspire in the causes and conditions that create our unhappiness and are often reluctant to engage in activities that could lead to more longlasting happiness. How can this be? In our normal way of life, we let ourselves be controlled by powerful thoughts and emotions, which in turn give rise to negative states of mind. It is by this vicious circle that we perpetuate not only our unhappiness but also that of others. We must deliberately take a stand to reverse these tendencies and replace them with new habits. Like a freshly grafted branch on an old tree that will eventually absorb the life of that tree and create a new one, we must nurture new inclinations by deliberately cultivating virtuous practices. This is the true meaning and object of the practice of meditation.

Contemplating the painful nature of life, considering the methods by which our misery can be brought to an end, is a form of meditation. This book is a form of meditation. The process by which we transform our more instinctual attitude to life, that state of mind which seeks only to satisfy desire and avoid discomforts, is what we mean when we use the word "meditation." We tend to be controlled by our mind, following it

along its self-centered path. Meditation is the process whereby
we gain control over the mind and guide it in a more virtuous direction. Meditation may be thought of as a technique
by which we diminish the force of old thought habits and develop new ones. We thereby protect ourselves from engaging in
actions of mind, word, or deed that lead to our suffering.

—*An Open Heart*, 45–46

In our practice of the Dharma, we seek to transcend the situation in which we all find ourselves: victims of our own mental
afflictions, the enemies of our peace and serenity. These afflictions — such as attachment, hatred, pride, greed, and so
forth — are mental states that cause us to behave in ways that
bring about all our unhappiness and suffering. While working
to achieve inner peace and happiness, it is helpful to think of
them as our inner demons, for like demons, they can haunt
us, causing nothing but misery. The state beyond such negative
emotions and thoughts, beyond all sorrow, is called nirvana.

Initially, it is impossible to combat these powerful negative forces directly. We must approach them gradually. We first
apply discipline; we refrain from becoming overwhelmed by
these emotions and thoughts. We do so by adopting an ethically
disciplined way of life....

We come to realize that extreme emotions such as attachment — and particularly anger and hatred — are very destructive when they arise in us and that they are also very destructive
when they arise in others! One could almost say that these emotions are the real destructive forces of the universe. We might
go further and say that most of the problems and suffering we
experience, which are essentially of our own making, are ultimately created by these negative emotions. One could say that
all suffering is in fact the result or fruit of negative emotions
such as attachment, greed, jealousy, pride, anger, and hatred.

Although at first we are not able to root out these negative emotions directly, at least we are not acting in accordance
with them. From here we move our meditative efforts to directly counter our afflictions of the mind and to deepen our
compassion. For the final stage of our journey we need to uproot our afflictions altogether. This necessitates a realization of
emptiness.   —*An Open Heart*, 79–80

Since the afflictive emotions contaminate karmas, or actions,
I will discuss them first. There are two classes of afflictive
emotions — one that is better expressed and the other that is
better not expressed. An example of the former is a terrible fear
from the past that becomes fixed in the mind. In this case, it
is definitely beneficial to let your feelings out and discuss the
incident. . . .

The other class of counterproductive emotions — which
include feelings such as lust, hatred, enmity, jealousy, and bel-
ligerence — should not be expressed; they become more and
more frequent. Expressing them tends to make them stronger
and more prevalent. It is better to reflect on the disadvantages
of engaging in such emotions and try to displace them with
feelings of satisfaction and love. We should forcefully overcome negative emotions when they appear, but it would be even
better to find ways to prevent them in the first place.

                                    —*How to Practice*, 43–45

You ask me what nirvana is. I would answer: a certain quality
of mind.   — *Violence and Compassion*, 135

The nature of the innermost subtle consciousness is pure. Anger,
attachment, and so forth are peripheral and do not subsist
in the basic mind. We call this the fundamental inborn mind
of clear light. Because it makes enlightenment possible, it is

also called the Buddha nature. It exists at the root of all consciousness. . . .

Pure from the start and endowed with a spontaneous nature, this diamond mind is the basis of all spiritual development. Even while generating a great many good and bad conceptions such as desire, hatred, and bewilderment, the diamond mind itself is free from the corruptions of these defilements, like sky throughout clouds. Water may be extremely dirty, yet its nature remains clear. Similarly, no matter what afflictive emotions are generated as the artifice of this diamond mind, and no matter how powerful they are, the basic mind itself remains unaffected by defilement; it is good without beginning or end.

— *How to Expand Love,* 20, 26

The Buddha nature is in each of us; it resides in every living creature and even in every atom. The impurities that we can accumulate in our different existences might obscure it, but they can't destroy it. As Nagarjuna wrote:

> As a metal ornament stained with impurity
> must be purified by fire,
> when it is placed in fire,
> the impurities are burned away, but not the ornament.
> In the same way in what concerns the mind
> whose nature is clear light,
> but which is soiled by the impurities of desire,
> the impurities are burned away by the fire of wisdom,
> but its nature, the clear light, remains.

So the mind, the greatest force in the universe, can escape all the contaminations, it can become better (or worse), it can lead to the Buddha-state by recognizing the Buddha nature that abides unchangeably in itself.

The Buddha nature is therefore a common individual potential to realize, but it is not in itself the Buddha-state. The Buddha-state is the end of all illusion, the cessation of all suffering, the knowledge of all the details of the world, the announcement that entry into nirvana is now possible. It is the point at which everything becomes clear and peaceful.

Shantideva describes the mind of awakening:

> It is the sublime nectar
> To destroy sovereign death,
> The inexhaustible treasure
> To eliminate the misery of the world.

Then the mind is reunited with the very mind of the Buddha, that substance called "subtle mind," which has no beginning or end, which is independent of the body and the brain and is undoubtedly the true cause of consciousness. This subtle mind, which is free of all attachments, has totally eliminated the obstacles that opposed the vision of "the ultimate nature of existence." — *Violence and Compassion,* 123–24

MEMENTO MORI: DEATH AS CATALYST FOR TRANSFORMATION

Before we can renounce cyclic existence, we must first recognize that we shall all inevitably die. We are born with the seed of our own death. From the moment of birth, we are approaching this inevitable demise. Then we must also contemplate that the time of our death is uncertain. Death does not wait for us to tidy up our lives. It strikes unannounced. At the time of our death, friends and family, the precious possessions we have so meticulously collected throughout our lives, are of no value. Not even this precious body, the vehicle of this lifetime, is of any use. Such thoughts help us diminish our preoccupation with the concerns of our present lives. They also begin to provide the groundwork for a compassionate understanding of how others find it difficult to let go of their self-centered concerns.

— An Open Heart, 39

Analysis of death is not for the sake of becoming fearful but to appreciate this precious lifetime during which you can perform many important practices.   *— Advice on Dying,* 39

When we contemplate death and the impermanence of life, our minds automatically begin to take an interest in spiritual achievements, just as an ordinary person becomes apprehensive upon seeing the corpse of a friend. Meditation upon impermanence and death is very useful, for it cuts off attraction toward transient and meaningless activities and causes the mind to turn toward the Dharma.

It is not difficult to recognize the certainty of death. The world is very old, but there is no sentient being we can point to who is immortal. The very nature of our body is vulnerability and impermanence. Beautiful or ugly, fat or thin, we all steadily approach death, and nothing can avert it. Physical power, flattery, bribery, and all the things of this world cannot persuade it to turn away.

On hearing that we have a fatal disease we run frantically from one doctor to another, and when that fails, we come to the lamas and ask them to do divinations to help us. Eventually we find ourselves eating our last meal, wearing our clothes for the last time, and sitting on our last seat. Then our body falls to the ground like a log.

Meditation upon death gives us a type of restlessness, an uneasiness, as though somebody dangerous were watching us.

This feeling is very real and useful, for, in truth, the certainty of death looms over us.

The time that death will strike is unknown to us. We do not know which will come first, tomorrow or the hereafter. None of us is able to guarantee that he or she will still be alive tonight. The slightest condition could cause us to have to suddenly part from this world. Even conditions that support life, such as food and medicine, can act as poisons and destroy one's life.

When we die, our body and all its powers are lost. Possessions, power, fame, and friends are all unable to accompany us. Take me, for example. Many Tibetans place a great deal of faith in me and would do anything I ask; but when I die I must die alone, and not one of them will be able to accompany me. All that one takes with one are knowledge of spiritual methods and karmic imprints of one's life deeds.

—*The Path to Enlightenment,* 87–88

It is better to decide from the very beginning that you will die and investigate what is worthwhile.   —*Advice on Dying,* 51

For us Buddhists, death is something very natural, a phenomenon that is part of the cycle of existence, *samsara.* Death is not an ending. It is something very familiar for us; we almost instinctively accept it, and we do not need to fear it. I imagine dying to be something like exchanging worn out clothes for new ones. This could be something wonderful.

—*Path of Wisdom, Path of Peace,* 120

We Buddhists believe that the deepest and most healing experiences can occur when we are dying.

—*Path of Wisdom, Path of Peace,* 124

APPROACHES AND METHODS

By recognizing that the mind is malleable, we can bring about changes to our attitudes by using different thought processes.
— An Open Heart, 19

In the case of anger and hatred, although they arise naturally, in order to dispel or overcome them we have to make a conscious decision and deliberately cultivate their antidotes, such as love and compassion. Because we gain from this endeavor we should engage in it.   *— Healing Anger,* 48

Meditation is needed in developing mental qualities. The mind is something that can definitely be transformed, and meditation is means to transform it. Meditation is the activity of familiarizing your mind, making it acquainted, with a new meaning. Basically it means getting used to the object on which you are meditating.

Meditation is of two types — analytical and stabilizing. First, an object is analyzed, after which the mind is set one-pointedly on the same object in stabilizing meditation. Within analytical meditation, there are also two types:

1. an object of meditation, such as impermanence, is taken as the object of the mind and one meditates on it;

2. a mental attitude is meditatively cultivated, as in cultivating love, in which case the mind becomes of the nature of the object meditated.   *— The Meaning of Life,* 4

The Tibetan word for meditation is *gom,* which means "to familiarize." When we use meditation on our spiritual path, it is to familiarize ourselves with a chosen object. This object need not be a physical thing such as an image of the Buddha or Jesus on the cross. The "chosen object" can be a mental quality such as patience, which we work at cultivating within ourselves by means of meditative contemplation. It can also be the rhythmic movement of our breath, which we focus on to still our restless minds. And it can be the mere quality of clarity and knowing — our consciousness — the nature of which we seek to understand....

For example, as we research what kind of car to buy, reading the pros and cons of different makes, we develop a sense of the qualities of a particular choice. By contemplating these qualities, our appreciation of this car intensifies, as does our desire to possess it. We can cultivate virtues such as patience and tolerance in much the same way. We do so by contemplating the qualities that constitute patience, the peace of mind it generates in us, the harmonious environment created as a result of it, the respect it engenders in others. We also work to recognize the drawbacks of impatience, the anger and lack of contentment we suffer within, the fear and hostility it brings about in those around us. When we diligently follow such lines of thought, our patience naturally evolves, growing stronger and stronger, day by day, month by month, year by year. The process of taming the mind is a lengthy one. Yet once we have mastered patience, the pleasure derived from it outlasts that provided by any car.

— *An Open Heart*, 50

Calm abiding meditation is a practice common to Buddhists and non-Buddhists. So in terms of its mere identity there is nothing profound or special about it. However, when we investigate the nature of some object, whether it is conventional or ultimate, calm abiding meditation is very important. Its main objective is to develop single-pointed concentration. Although we say prayers or engage in tantric practices, we are faced with the question of whether they are effective. The main reason is our lack of concentration. So, we should develop a mind that is able to abide single-pointedly on the object of focus. In the initial stages, even if we are unable to generate a final calmly abiding mind, it is crucial to cultivate a good deal of mental stability while practicing the six perfections, altruistic ideals, and so forth. The final goal of practicing calm abiding meditation is to actualize special insight.   — *Stages of Meditation,* 120–21

Generally speaking, we can point to two types of emotion. One is more instinctual and is not based on reason. The other type of emotion — such as compassion or tolerance — is not so instinctual but instead has a sound base or grounding in reason and experience. When you clearly see the various logical grounds for their development and you develop conviction in these benefits, then these emotions will be enhanced. What we see here is a joining of intellect and heart. Compassion represents the emotion, the heart, and the application of analytic meditation applies the intellect. So when you have arrived at that meditative state where compassion is enhanced, you see a special merging of intellect and heart.   — *The Good Heart,* 47

As we analyze our mental experiences, we recognize that the powerful emotions we possess (such as desire, hatred, and anger) tend not to bring us very profound or long-lasting happiness. Fulfilled desire may provide a sense of temporary satisfaction; however, the pleasure we experience upon acquiring a new car or home, for example, is usually short-lived. When we indulge in our desires, they tend to increase in intensity and multiply in number. We become more demanding and less content, finding it more difficult to satisfy our needs. In the Buddhist view, hatred, anger, and desire are afflictive emotions, which simply means they tend to cause us discomfort. The discomfort arises from the mental unease that follows the expression of these emotions. . . .

If we continue to accommodate them, they will grow stronger, exerting greater and greater influence over us. Spiritual practice, then, is a process of taming these emotions and diminishing their force. For ultimate happiness to be attained, they must be removed totally.   *—An Open Heart, 33*

For a Dharma practitioner, one of the major challenges is to counter our disturbing emotions and finally free ourselves from them. The difficulty of this is due to the simple truth that disturbing emotions have from beginningless time caused us to suffer all kinds of miseries. If someone bullies us or an enemy persecutes us, then we raise a hue and cry. External enemies, however brutal they are, only affect us during one lifetime. They have no power to harm us beyond this life. On the other hand, disturbing emotions are our inner enemies and can definitely cause disaster in future lives. These are, in fact, our worst enemies.

The real test for a Dharma practitioner comes from this angle: if our disturbing emotions are reduced, then our practice has been effective. This is the main criterion in determining a true practitioner, regardless of how holy we appear externally. The whole purpose of meditation is to lessen the deluded afflictions of our mind and eventually eradicate them from their very roots. By learning and practicing the profound and the vast aspects of the teaching, a practitioner with prolonged familiarity with and meditation on selflessness eventually gains an understanding of reality.   *—Stages of Meditation, 21*

Let us do a meditation with a little bit of visualization. Imagine a scenario where someone that you know very well, someone who is close or dear to you, loses his or her temper, either in a very acrimonious relationship, or in a situation where something else is happening. This person shows all signs of being in an intense state of anger or hatred, loses all mental composure,

creates very negative "vibes," even goes to the extent of harming himself or herself and breaking things. Then reflect upon the
immediate effects of intense anger or hatred. The reason why I
think we should visualize this happening to others is because it
is easier to see the faults of others than to see our own faults. So
visualize this, and even see a physical transformation happening to that person. This person whom you feel close to, whom
you like, the very sight of whom gave you pleasure in the past,
now turns into this ugly, ugly person, even physically speaking.
This is a kind of analytic meditation, so do this meditation and
visualization for a few minutes, in an analytical way, using your
imaginative faculty. At the end of it, relate that to your own experience. Then resolve, "I shall never let myself fall under the
sway of such intense anger and hatred. Because if I do that,
I will also be in the same position and suffer all these consequences — lose my peace of mind, lose my composure, assume
this ugly physical appearance, and so on." Make that decision,
and then remain in an absorptive meditation on this conclusion.
                                                    — *Healing Anger,* 44

Patiently accepting small hardships also gives one the opportunity to apply other practices. One could make the aspirational
prayers and the dedication, "By my experience of this suffering,
may I be able to purify my negativities committed in the past."
One can also use the opportunity for the practice of *tong-len,*
which is the Mahayana practice of "giving and taking." For
that, when one undergoes the experience of pain and suffering
one thinks, "May my suffering substitute for all similar types
of suffering that sentient beings may have to undergo. May I,
by experiencing this, be able to save all other sentient beings
from having to undergo the same suffering." So in this way one
takes others' suffering upon oneself and uses the experience of
hardship as an opportunity for this type of practice as well.

This advice is especially useful when dealing with illnesses. ...Although it may not succeed in alleviating the real physical pain and suffering, one can think, "May I, by experiencing this pain and suffering, be able to help other people and save others who may have to go through the same experience." One can in this way use that opportunity for a spiritual practice, in other words, practicing *tong-len* meditation, or "giving and taking." This type of practice, although it might not necessarily lead to a real cure in physical terms, can definitely protect one from unnecessary additional mental suffering and pain. And on top of that, it is also possible that instead of being saddened by the experience one can see it as a kind of privilege. One can see it as an opportunity and in fact be joyful because of this particular experience which has made one's life richer.

—*Healing Anger,* 78–79

EQUANIMITY AND IMPARTIALITY

If you see that some situation or person is going to cause you suffering, it is important to engage in techniques to avoid it; but once suffering has started, it should be received not as a burden but as something that can assist you. Undergoing small sufferings in this lifetime can purify the karma of many ill deeds accumulated in former lifetimes. Adopting this perspective will help you see the ills of cyclic existence, and the more you do this, the more you will dislike engaging in nonvirtues. Hardship also helps you to see the advantages of liberation. In addition, through your own experience of suffering, you will be able to empathize with the pain of others and generate a wish to do something for them. So, seen in this way, suffering can provide a remarkable opportunity for more practice and more thought.

From this viewpoint, enemies are teachers of inner strength, courage, and determination. This does not mean you should give in to those who would harm you. Depending on the enemy's attitude, you may have to defend yourself strongly, but deep down try to maintain your calm by realizing that, like you, she is a person who wants happiness and does not want suffering. It is hard to believe, but over time, it is possible to develop such an attitude. Here is how to do it:

> Consider the so-called enemy. Because this person's mind is untamed, she engages in activities to bring injury to you. If anger — the wish to harm — were in the very nature of the person, it could not be altered in any way, but...hatred does not subsist in the nature of a person. And even if it were the nature of a person, then just as we cannot get angry at fire because it burns our hand (it is the very nature of fire to burn), so should we not get angry at a person expressing her nature. This said, hatred is actually peripheral to a person's nature. Thus, just as when a cloud covers the sun, we do not get angry at the sun, so we should not get angry at the so-called enemy but instead hold the person's afflictive emotion responsible.
>
> We ourselves sometimes engage in bad behavior, do we not? Still, most of us do not think we are completely bad. We should look on others the same way. The actual troublemaker is not the person, but his or her afflictive emotion.

When we lose our temper, we have no hesitation about speaking harsh words even to a close friend. Afterward, when we cool down, we feel embarrassed about what happened. This indicates that we, as persons, do not want to use such harsh words, but because we lost our power and were dominated by anger, something happened outside our control. One day my driver in Tibet was working under my car and bumped his head against the chassis; he got so angry, he hit his head against the car a couple of times as if to punish the vehicle, but of course he hurt himself instead. . . .

We can learn to separate a corner of the mind from strong emotions like hatred and watch it; this indicates that the mind and hatred are not one; the person and hatred are not one.

—How to Expand Love, 67–69

We often confuse the actions of a person with the actual person. This habit leads us to conclude that because of a particular action or statement, a person is our enemy. Yet people are neutral. They are neither friend nor enemy, Buddhist nor Christian, Chinese nor Tibetan. As a result of circumstances, the person we hold in our sights could change and become our closest friend. The thought "Oh, you used to be so mean to me in the past, but now we are such good friends" is not inconceivable.

Another way of cultivating equanimity and transcending our feelings of partiality and discrimination is to reflect upon how we are all equal in our aspiration to be happy and overcome suffering. Additionally, we all feel that we have a basic right to fulfill this aspiration. How do we justify this right? Very simply, it is part of our fundamental nature. I am not unique; I have no special privilege. You are not unique, nor do you hold special privileges. My aspiration to be happy and overcome suffering is part of my fundamental nature, as it is a part of yours. If this is so, then just as we do, all others have the right to be happy and overcome suffering, simply because they share this fundamental nature. It is on the basis of this equality that we develop equanimity toward all. In our meditation we must work at cultivating the attitude that "just as I myself have the desire to be happy and overcome suffering, so do all others, and just as I have the natural right to fulfill this aspiration, so do all others." We should repeat this thought as we meditate and as we go about our lives, until it sinks deep into our awareness.

There is one last consideration. As human beings, our well-being very much depends upon that of others, and our very survival is the result of contributions made by many, many beings. Our birth is dependent upon our parents. We then need their care and affection for a number of years. Our livelihood, our dwelling, our sustenance, even our success and fame, are the result of contributions made by innumerable fellow human beings. Whether directly or indirectly, countless others are involved in our survival—not to mention our happiness.

If we extend this line of reasoning beyond the confines of a single lifetime, we can imagine that throughout our previous lives—in fact, since time without beginning—countless others have made innumerable contributions to our welfare. We conclude, "What grounds have I to discriminate? How can I be close to some and hostile toward others? I must rise above feelings of partiality and discrimination. I must be benefit to all, equally!"
                                                    —*An Open Heart*, 113–15

So I think this mental practice is to look at [things] in a holistic way, to see that there are many events involved. We cannot pinpoint responsibility for what happened entirely on one person. As another example, consider our problem with the Chinese. I think many contributions were made from the Tibetan side that led to this tragic situation. Perhaps our generation made some contributions, but definitely the previous generations did, for at least a few generations' time. So it is not fair to blame everything on China.

So if we examine any given situation in an unbiased and honest way, and also from a wide perspective, then we realize that, to a large extent, we are also responsible for the unfolding of events.
                                                    —*Healing Anger*, 57

Forgiveness is something like an end result, or a product, of patience or tolerance. When one is truly patient and tolerant, then forgiveness comes naturally. So they are very intimately connected.   — *Healing Anger,* 64

Destruction of your enemy is destruction of yourself.
                                               — *How to See Yourself,* 9

How do we train our minds to perceive the essential equality of all living beings? It is best to cultivate the feeling of equanimity by first focusing on relative strangers or acquaintances, those for whom you have no strong feeling one way or another. From there you should meditate impartially, moving on to friends and then enemies. Upon achieving an impartial attitude toward all sentient beings, you should meditate on love, the wish that they find the happiness they seek.

The seed of compassion will grow if you plant it in fertile soil, a consciousness moistened with love. When you have watered your mind in love, you can begin to meditate upon compassion. Compassion, here, is simply the wish that all sentient beings be free of suffering.   — *An Open Heart,* 115

ON MOTHERS AS SOURCE
OF MEDITATION

If we have been reborn time after time, it is evident that we have needed many mothers to give birth to us. It should be mentioned that our births have not been limited to the planet Earth. According to the Buddhist view, we have been going through the cycle of life and death for far longer than our planet has existed. Our past lives are therefore infinite, as are the beings who have given birth to us. Thus, the first cause bringing about *bodhicitta* [the

resolve for awakening for the benefit of all sentient creatures] is
the recognition that all beings have been our mother.

The love and kindness shown us by our mother in this life
would be difficult to repay. She endured many sleepless nights to
care for us when we were helpless infants. She fed us and would
have willingly sacrificed everything, including her own life, to
spare ours. As we contemplate her example of devoted love, we
should consider that each and every being throughout existence
has treated us this way. Each dog, cat, fish, fly, and human being
has at some point in the beginningless past been our mother
and shown us overwhelming love and kindness. Such a thought
should bring about our appreciation. This is the second cause
of *bodhicitta.*

As we envision the present condition of all these beings, we
begin to develop the desire to help them change their lot. This
is the third cause, and out of it comes the fourth, a feeling of
love cherishing all beings. This is an attraction toward all beings,
similar to what a child feels upon seeing his or her mother. This
leads us to compassion, which is the fifth cause of *bodhicitta.*
Compassion is a wish to separate these suffering beings, our
mothers of the past, from their miserable situation. At this point
we also experience loving-kindness, a wish that all beings find
happiness. As we progress through these stages of responsibility,
we go from wishing that all sentient beings find happiness and
freedom from suffering to personally assuming responsibility for
helping them enter this state beyond misery. This is the final cause.
As we scrutinize how best to help others, we are drawn to achieve
the fully enlightened and omniscient state of Buddhahood.

The implicit question in this method is central to Mahayana
Buddhism: if all other sentient beings who have been kind to
us since beginningless time are suffering, how can we devote
ourselves to pursuing merely our own happiness? To seek our
own happiness in spite of the suffering others are experiencing

is tragically unfortunate. Therefore, it is clear that we must try to free all sentient beings from suffering. This method helps us cultivate the desire to do so.   —*An Open Heart,* 120–22

We should ensure that whatever we do, we maintain some effect or influence from our meditation so that it directs our actions as we live our everyday lives. By our doing so, everything we do outside our formal sessions becomes part of our training in compassion. It is not difficult for us to develop sympathy for a child in the hospital or an acquaintance mourning the death of a spouse. We must start to consider how to keep our hearts open toward those we would normally envy, those who enjoy fine lifestyles and wealth. With an ever deeper recognition of what suffering is, gained from our meditation sessions, we become able to relate to such people with compassion. Eventually, we should be able to relate to all beings this way, seeing that their situation is always dependent upon the conditions of the vicious cycle of life. In this way all interactions with others become catalysts for deepening our compassion. This is how we keep our hearts open in our daily lives, outside our formal meditation periods.

True compassion has the intensity and spontaneity of a loving mother caring for her suffering baby. Throughout the day, such a mother's concern for her child affects all her thoughts and actions. This is the attitude we are working to cultivate toward each and every being. When we experience this, we have generated "great compassion."   —*An Open Heart,* 104–5

EXCHANGING SELF FOR OTHERS

The other method for bringing about *bodhicitta,* the aspiration to attain highest enlightenment for the sake of all sentient creatures, is Exchanging Self for Others. In this method, we work at recognizing how dependent we are on others for all we have. We contemplate how the homes we live in, the clothes we wear, the roads we drive on, have all been created by the hard work of others. So much work has gone into providing us with the shirt we are wearing, from planting the cottonseed to weaving the fabric and sewing the garment. The slice of bread we eat had to be baked by someone. The wheat had to be planted by someone else and, after irrigation and fertilization, had to be harvested and then milled into flour. This had to be kneaded into dough and then baked appropriately. It would be impossible to count all the people involved in providing us with a simple slice of bread. In many cases machines do a lot of the work; however, they had to be invented and produced, and must be supervised. Even our personal virtues, such as our patience and ethical sense, are all developed in dependence upon others. We can even come to appreciate that those who cause us difficulty are providing us with the opportunity to develop tolerance. Through this train of thought we come to recognize how dependent we are on others for all we enjoy in life. We must work at developing this recognition as we go about our lives after our morning meditation sessions. There are so many examples of our dependence on others. As we recognize them, our sense of responsibility toward others develops, as does our desire to repay them for their kindness.

—*An Open Heart,* 122–23

MINDFULNESS

Whether we talk of the transformation of consciousness or of the introspective empirical analysis of what occurs in the mind, the observer needs a range of skills, carefully honed through repetition and training, and applied in a rigorous and disciplined manner. All these practices assume a certain ability to direct one's mind to a chosen object and to hold the attention there for a period, however brief. An assumption is also made that, through constant habituation, the mind learns to improve the quality of whatever faculty is being applied, whether it is attention, reasoning, or imagination. The understanding is that through such prolonged and regular practice, the ability to perform the exercise will become almost second nature. Here the parallel with athletes or musicians is very clear, but one might equally think of learning how to swim or how to ride a bicycle. Initially, these are very difficult, seemingly unnatural activities, but once you master the skills, they come quite easily.

One of the most basic mental trainings is the cultivation of mindfulness, especially performed on the basis of observing one's breath. Mindfulness is essential if one is to become consciously aware in a disciplined manner of whatever phenomena may occur within the mind or one's immediate environment. In our normal state, our mind remains unfocused for most of the time and our thoughts move from one object to another in a random and dissipated manner. By cultivating mindfulness, we learn first to become aware of this process of dissipation, so that we can gently fine-tune the mind to follow a more directed path toward the objects on which we wish to focus. Traditionally, the breath is seen as an ideal instrument for the practice of mindfulness. The great advantage of choosing one's breath as the object of mindfulness training is that breathing is an instinctive and effortless activity, something which we do as long as we are alive, so there is no need to strive hard to find the object of this practice. In its developed form, mindfulness also brings about a highly refined sensitivity to everything that happens, however minute, in one's immediate vicinity and in one's mind.

— *The Universe in a Single Atom,* 151

PERSPECTIVES

For people who have the problem of self-hatred or self-loathing, for the time being it is advisable that they not think seriously about the suffering nature of existence or the underlying unsatisfactory nature of existence. Rather they should concentrate on the positive aspects of existence, such as appreciating the potentials that lie within oneself as a human being, the opportunities that one's existence as a human being affords. In the traditional teaching, one speaks about all the qualities of a fully endowed human existence. By reflecting upon these opportunities and potentials, one will be able to increase one's sense of worth and confidence.   — *Healing Anger,* 66

What is the Bodhisattva's way of life? It is the way of life that follows naturally from having cultivated the awakening mind of *bodhicitta.* Omniscience is achieved only through the process of purifying the disturbing emotions within your mind. It cannot be achieved merely through wishes and prayers. We have to train in eliminating all the specific disturbing emotions by relying on specific antidotes. All the activities of a Bodhisattva can be included in two major categories: the practice of skillful means and the practice of wisdom. If the practices of giving, ethics, and so forth are to be perfected, they should be supported and influenced by the practice of wisdom. Without the practice of wisdom, the first five of the six perfections (giving, ethics, patience, effort, meditation, wisdom) cannot become practices of perfection....

However, even when you have understood the wisdom realizing emptiness, that alone will not become a powerful antidote to ignorance if it is not supported by other practices such as giving, ethics, patience, and so forth. Mere understanding of selflessness is not sufficient to defeat the disturbing emotions.

Therefore, it is important to cultivate a practice that unites a calmly abiding mind with special insight. In order to develop special insight you must first develop a calmly abiding mind. Calm abiding is single-pointed meditation, whereas special insight refers to discriminative awareness. Through the union of these two, you will be able to engage in a fruitful practice of both method and wisdom.   —*Stages of Meditation*, 76–77

The fundamental teaching of Buddha is that we should view others as being more important than we are. Of course, you cannot completely ignore yourself. But neither can you neglect the welfare of other people and other sentient beings, particularly when there is a clash of interest between your own welfare and the welfare of other people. At such a time you should consider other people's welfare as more important than your own personal well-being. Compare yourself to the rest of sentient beings. All other sentient beings are countless, while you are just one person. Your suffering and happiness may be very important, but it is just the suffering and happiness of one individual, whereas the happiness and suffering of all other sentient beings is immeasurable and countless. So, it is the way of the wise to sacrifice one for the benefit of the majority and it is the way of the foolish to sacrifice the majority on behalf of just one single individual. Even from the point of view of your personal well-being, you must cultivate a compassionate mind — that is the source of happiness in your life.

—*Stages of Meditation*, 71–72

4

Religions and the World

One of the compelling virtues of the Dalai Lama is his intel-
lectual curiosity. This quality is longstanding in him, shown in
reflections on his youth that he captures in his autobiography,
Freedom in Exile. *As a young boy, he became friends with the*
*German mountaineer Heinrich Harrer (*Seven Years in Tibet*),*
whom the Dalai Lama would pepper with questions about the
West. This congenital curiosity has carried over into adulthood,
as he has convened or participated in numerous conferences and
opportunities to bring together scholars, thinkers, and religious
leaders. These opportunities serve not only to engage a rich
and healthy dialogue among the world's best minds but also
to enhance his own understanding of a particular topic, such
as quantum physics, Western theories of consciousness, Chris-
tian theology and monasticism, or the relationship that obtains
between the world's religions.

What is striking about these inquiries is that they also seem
motivated in part by personal relationship or encounter with
non-Buddhists. For example, he repeatedly has mentioned the
positive impact Thomas Merton made on him as he came to
understand and appreciate the values of Christian monasticism
and theology. In short, the Dalai Lama seems genuinely to

enjoy a rich set of relationships characterized by curiosity, empathy, and friendliness. In fact, most people who see or meet the Dalai Lama cannot help but be struck by his warmth, affability, and good humor — along with a humility that includes gentle self-deprecation. This impression makes all the more jarring Chinese representations of him as a cynical politician. Indeed, it must be remembered that in the uprisings in Lhasa in the spring of 2008, the Dalai Lama threatened to resign his political office. The occasion for this threat, however, was not the violence of the Chinese against Tibetans, but the Tibetan option of violence against the Chinese. This choice, far from being "Machiavellian," in fact reveals the deepest current of his spirituality, namely, compassion for all beings. And for compassion to be genuine, authentic, and real, it must be unconditional. The so-called enemy is a phenomenon that arises in a particular context; it has nothing to do with any essential characteristic or intrinsic nature. Enemies are human beings with needs and longings, sufferings and anguish, the hope for freedom and well-being shared by all people. They deserve happiness no less than anyone else. In the end, the greatest opportunity and test of our spiritual practice is precisely to love our enemy. While religions often suffer intractable philosophical differences, this trajectory of love, for the Dalai Lama, is the ultimate and most meaningful meeting ground of the religions of the world.

PREMISES

Developing a kind heart, a feeling of closeness for all beings, does not require following a conventional religious practice. It is not only for those who believe in religion. It is for everyone, regardless of race, religion, or political affiliation. It is for all who consider themselves to be, above all, members of the human family, who can embrace this larger and longer perspective. The basic values of love and compassion are present in us from the time of our birth, whereas racial, ethnic, political, and theological perspectives come later. Violence does not accord with our basic human nature, which may lead you to wonder why all sorts of violence become the news but compassionate acts seldom do. The reason is that violence is shocking and not in conformity with our basic human nature, whereas we take compassionate acts for granted because they are closer to our nature.   — *How to See Yourself*, 12

ON RELIGIONS

There are many religions that set forth precepts and advice on how to adjust one's mental attitude, and all, without exception, are concerned with making the mind more peaceful, disciplined, moral, and ethical. In this way, the essence of all religion is the same, even though in terms of philosophy there are many differences.   — *The Heart of Compassion*, 103

Although, in every religion, there is an emphasis on compassion and love, from the viewpoint of philosophy, there are differences, and that is all right. Philosophical teachings are not the end, not the aim, not what you serve. The aim is to help and benefit others, and philosophical teachings that support those ideas are valuable. If we go into the differences in philosophy and argue with and criticize each other, it is useless. There will be endless argument; the only result will be that we irritate each other — accomplishing nothing. It is better to look at the purpose of the philosophies and to see what is shared — an emphasis on love, compassion, and respect for a higher force.
                                          — *Policy of Kindness*, 55

I have come to see that all traditions have great potential and can play a very important role in benefiting humanity. All the world religions contain tools to address our basic aspiration to overcome suffering and increase happiness....

Some religions have sophisticated philosophical analyses; some have extensive ethical teachings; some place a greater emphasis on faith. If we observe the teachings of the world's major faith traditions, however, we can discern two main dimensions of religion. One is what would be called the metaphysical or philosophical dimension, which explains why we are the way we are and why certain religious practices are prescribed. The second dimension pertains to the practice of morality or ethical discipline. One could say that the ethical teachings of a faith tradition are the conclusions supported and validated by the process of the metaphysical or philosophical thinking. Although the world's religions differ widely in terms of metaphysics and philosophy, the conclusions these differing philosophies arrive at — that is, their ethical teachings — show a high degree of convergence. In this sense, we can say that regardless of whatever metaphysical explanations religious traditions employ, they all reach similar conclusions. In some form or other, the philosophies of all the world religions emphasize love, compassion, tolerance, forgiveness, and the importance of self-discipline. Through interfaith and interpersonal communication, sharing, and respect, we can learn to appreciate the valuable qualities taught by all religions, and the ways in which all religions can benefit humanity.

Within each path, we can find people who are truly dedicated to the welfare of others out of a deep sense of compassion and love. Over the past few decades, I've met quite a number of people from many different traditions — Christians, Hindus, Muslims, and Jews. And within every tradition, one finds wonderful, warm-hearted, sensible people — people like

Mother Teresa, who completely dedicated her life to the well-being of the poorest of the world's poor, and Dr. Martin Luther King Jr., who dedicated his life to the peaceful struggle for equality. Clearly, all traditions have the power to bring out the best in human potential. Yet different traditions use different approaches.

Now, we may ask, "Why is this so? Why is there such metaphysical and philosophical diversity among the world's religions?" Such diversity can be found not only among different religions but also *within* religions as well. Even within Buddhism — even within the teachings of Buddha Shakyamuni himself — there is a great diversity of teachings. In Buddha's more philosophical teachings, we find this diversity to be most pronounced; in some cases, the teachings seem even to contradict one another!

This points, I think, to one of the most important truths about spiritual teachings: spiritual teachings must be appropriate to the individual being taught. The Buddha recognized among his followers a diversity of mental dispositions, spiritual inclinations, and interests, and saw that in order to suit this diversity he had to teach differently in different contexts. No matter how powerful a particular teaching may be or how "correct" a philosophical view may be, if it is not suitable to the individual hearing it, it has no value. A skillful spiritual teacher will thus judge the appropriateness of a given teaching for a given individual and teach accordingly.

We can draw an analogy to the use of medicine. Antibiotics, for instance, are immensely powerful; they are immensely valuable in treating a wide variety of diseases — but they are useless in treating a broken leg. A broken leg must be set in a cast. Furthermore, even in cases where antibiotics are indeed the appropriate treatment, if a doctor were to give an infant the same amount of medicine as she would a fully grown man, the child might die!

In the same way, we can see that the Buddha himself — because he recognized the diversity of mental dispositions, interests, and mental capacities of his followers — gave diverse teachings. Looking at all the world's religions in this light, I feel a deep conviction that all of the traditions are beneficial, each of them uniquely serving the needs of their followers.

Let's look at the similarities another way. Not all religions posit the existence of God, of a creator; but those that do emphasize that the devout should love God with all their heart. How might we determine whether someone loves God sincerely? Surely, we would examine that person's behavior and attitude toward fellow human beings, toward the rest of God's creation. If someone shows genuine love and compassion toward fellow human brothers and sisters, and toward the Earth itself, then I think we can be sure that that person truly demonstrates love for God. It's clear that when someone really respects God's message, they emulate God's love for humanity. Conversely, I believe that the faith of someone who professes belief in God and yet shows no love or compassion toward other human beings is highly questionable. When we look in these ways, we see that genuine faith in God is a powerful way to develop the positive human qualities of love and compassion.

Let's look at another differing aspect of world religions: belief in a previous life or a next life. Not all religions assert the existence of these things.... According to the Christian view, this life, the present life right now, has been created directly by God. I can well imagine that if we really believe this sincerely, it would grant a feeling of deep intimacy with God. Surely, being aware that our very lives are God's creation, we would develop a profound reverence for God and the wish to live our lives thoroughly in accord with God's intentions, thereby actualizing our highest human potential.

Other religions or people may emphasize that we are each responsible for everything we create in our lives. This kind of faith can also be very effective in helping to actualize our potential for goodness, for it requires that individuals take total responsibility for their lives, with all the consequences resting on their own shoulders. People who genuinely think in this way will become more disciplined, and take on full responsibility for practicing compassion and love. So while the approach is different, the result is more or less the same.

— Essence of the Heart Sutra, 9–13

In this world, just as there are many medicines for a particular disease, so there are many religious systems that serve as methods for achieving happiness for all sentient beings, human and otherwise.   *— The Buddhism of Tibet, 16*

I believe that when we seriously follow the teachings of our religion day after day, our overall attitude toward life gradually begins to change. Especially in times of need and crisis, religion can give people trust and confidence, no matter how bad the circumstances may be. Religion shows that despite all the sorrowful experiences there is still an indestructible ultimate meaning. In a mysterious way, religion gives humanity the gift of a hope stronger than all obstacles, than all afflictions.

— Path of Wisdom, Path of Peace, 69

Perhaps the most significant obstruction to interreligious harmony is lack of appreciation of the value of others' faith traditions....

I believe that the best way to overcome ignorance and bring about an understanding is through dialogue with members of other faith traditions. This I see occurring in a number of different ways. Discussions among scholars in which the convergence and perhaps more importantly the divergence between faith traditions are explored and appreciated are very valuable. On another level, it is helpful when there are encounters between ordinary but practicing followers of different religions in which each shares their experiences. This is perhaps the most effective way of appreciating others' teachings. In my own case, for example, my meetings with the late Thomas Merton, a Catholic monk of the Cistercian order, were deeply inspiring. They helped me develop a profound admiration for the teachings of Christianity. I also feel that occasional meetings between religious leaders joining together to pray for a common cause are extremely useful. The gathering at Assisi in Italy in 1986, when representatives of the world's major religions gathered to pray for peace, was, I believe, tremendously beneficial to many religious believers insofar as it symbolized the solidarity and a commitment to peace of all those taking part.

Finally, I feel that the practice of members of different faith traditions going on joint pilgrimages together can be very helpful. It was in this spirit that in 1993 I went to Lourdes, and then to Jerusalem, a site holy to three of the world's great religions. I have also paid visits to various Hindu, Islamic, Jain, and Sikh shrines both in India and abroad. More recently, following a seminar devoted to discussing and practicing meditation in the Christian and Buddhist traditions, I joined a historic pilgrimage of practitioners of both traditions in a program of prayers, meditation, and dialogue under the Bodhi tree at Bodh Gaya in India. This is one of Buddhism's most important shrines.

When exchanges like these occur, followers of one tradition will find that, just as in the case of their own, the teachings of others' faiths are a source both of spiritual inspiration and ethical guidance to their followers. It will also become clear that irrespective of doctrinal and other differences, all the major world religions are concerned with helping individuals to become good human beings. All emphasize love and compassion, patience, tolerance, forgiveness, humility, and so on, and all are capable of helping individuals to develop these.

— *Ethics for the New Millennium*, 222–23

CHRISTIANS, CHRISTIAN BELIEFS, AND BUDDHISM

Mother Teresa is an exemplar of how much someone can do with spiritual power. I met her in 1988 at the airport in Delhi. I was especially impressed with her humility. From the Buddhist perspective, Mother Teresa is certainly a Bodhisattva. She dedicated her life exclusively to the poor, which is truly living the Christian faith. I do not know that I would be capable of doing what she did.   — *Path of Wisdom, Path of Peace*, 76

When we come across a part of society that is in a particularly miserable situation, it is a good opportunity to exercise our sense of concern, of caring and compassion. However, I often tell people, "My compassion is just empty words. The late Mother Teresa really implemented compassion!"

— *An Open Heart*, 23

I became acquainted with Thomas Merton in 1968 in Dharamsala, shortly before his death. Even today, he embodies Christianity for me. Thomas Merton was a deeply religious man and full of humility. I had never experienced such spirituality in a Christian. For me, Thomas Merton was a Catholic *Geshe*, an especially learned monk. In the conversations with him, I discovered that many things are similar in Buddhism and Catholicism. Later I also met with Christians who radiated a similar quality. But this Trappist monk was the first who showed me what it means to be a Christian.

It is impressive how Christians of all denominations throughout the world offer practical help in many relief organizations. This is where we Buddhists can learn from Christians. In terms of meditation, I found it astonishing that body posture is not important in Christianity. In Buddhist meditation, the seated posture and breathing are key elements. Christians could certainly learn much from our meditation techniques.

— Path of Wisdom, Path of Peace, 77

I've asked many different Christian practitioners and Christian priests about [the rejection of the belief in reincarnation]. I was told by all of them, quite unanimously, that this belief in rebirth is not accepted in Christian doctrine — although no specific reason was given as to why the concept of rebirth would not fit in the wider context of Christian faith and practice. However, about two years ago in Australia, at my last meeting with Father Bede Griffiths (I have met him on several occasions and know him personally), I asked him the same question. I vividly remember the meeting; he was dressed in his *sadhu* saffron-yellow robes, and it was a very moving encounter. He said that, from the Christian point of view, a belief in rebirth would undermine the force in one's faith and practice. When you accept that this life, your individual existence, has been directly created and is like a direct gift from the Creator, it immediately creates a very special bond between you as an individual creature and the Creator. There's a direct personal connection that gives you a sense of closeness and an intimacy with your Creator. A belief in rebirth would undermine that special relationship with the Creator. I found this explanation deeply convincing.   *— The Good Heart,* 58–59

When I give Buddhist teachings to Western people of different religious backgrounds, I usually feel a little apprehensive.
It's not my wish to propagate Buddhism. At the same time, it
is quite natural that out of millions of people, some may feel
that the Buddhist approach is more suitable for them, more
effective for them. And even if an individual feeling this way
gets to the point where he or she is considering adopting the
Buddha's teachings, it is still very important to examine those
teachings and that decision carefully. Only after thinking very
deeply, examining very thoroughly, can one really determine
that the Buddhist approach is, in one's own case, more suitable
and effective.   — *Essence of the Heart Sutra,* 14–15

Of course, there are many common elements among all major
world religious traditions. Therefore, I believe, at the initial
stage one person can practice both Buddhism and Christianity
simultaneously. . . . I think this is very good.

But the question is when one reaches further. Then it is like
in the field of education: when one becomes a specialist, then
one has to choose a particular field. In the further practice
of Buddhism, when one reaches a certain stage, the realization of emptiness is one of the key aspects of the path. The
concept of emptiness and the concept of an absolute Creator
I think are difficult to put together. On the other hand, for
the Christian practitioner, the Creator and the acceptance of
the Creator as almighty is a very important factor within that
tradition in order to develop self-discipline, compassion, or forgiveness and to increase them in one's intimate relationship with
God. That's something very essential. In addition, when God is
seen as absolute and almighty, the concept that everything is
relative becomes a little bit difficult. However, if one's understanding of God is in terms of an ultimate nature of reality
or ultimate truth, then it is possible to have a kind of unified

approach. Then if we try to make a new interpretation, the concept of Father, Son, and Holy Ghost I think might be compared to the *sambhogakaya, nirmanakaya,* and *dharmakaya,* the three *kayas* (i.e., the three "bodies" or manifestations of the Buddha as an impersonal ultimate truth of reality [the Buddha nature of reality or *dharmakaya*], as celestial Buddha's presiding over heavenly domains [*sambhogakaya*], as a magical apparition [*nirmanakaya*] in the form of the Buddha of this age, Siddhartha Gautama. The celestial Buddhas and Siddhartha, on this view, are no more real than anything else, but are manifestations emerging from the ultimate Buddha nature out of compassion to help sentient beings.) However, once one begins to interpret the Trinity in terms such as the three-kaya doctrine, then whether that practice truly remains Christian becomes quite questionable.

As to one's personal religion, I think this must be based on one's own mental disposition. That is very important. So I tell people that as a Buddhist monk I find Buddhism most suitable to me. This does not mean Buddhism is best for everyone. For other people, the Christian, Muslim, or Jewish tradition, a tradition which is based on Creator theory, is more effective, that's certain. . . .

Generally speaking, I think it is better to practice according to your own traditional background, and certainly you can use some of the Buddhist techniques. Without accepting rebirth theory or the complicated philosophy, simply use certain techniques to increase your power of patience and compassion, forgiveness.   — *Healing Anger,* 69–70

Personally, when I look at the idea of Creation and the belief in a divine Creator, I feel that the main effect of that belief is to give a sense of motivation — a sense of urgency in the individual practitioner's commitment to becoming a good human being, an ethically disciplined person. When you have such a concept or belief, it also gives you a sense of purpose in your existence. It is very helpful in developing moral principles.

That is my understanding of Christian theology!

— *The Good Heart*, 56

Actually, the business of identifying *tulkus* is more logical than it may first appear. Given the Buddhist belief that the principle of rebirth is fact, and given that the whole purpose of reincarnation is to enable a being to continue its efforts on behalf of all suffering sentient beings, it stands to reason that it should be possible to identify individual cases. This enables them to be educated and placed in the world so that they can continue their work as soon as possible....

As I have said, the whole purpose of reincarnation is to facilitate the continuity of a being's work. This fact has great implications when it comes to searching for the successor of a particular person. For example, while my efforts in general are directed toward helping all sentient beings, in particular they are directed toward helping my fellow Tibetans. Therefore, if I die before Tibetans regain their freedom, it is only logical to assume that I will be born outside Tibet. Of course, it could be that by then my people will have no use for a Dalai Lama, in which case they will not bother to search for me. So I might take rebirth as an insect, or an animal — whatever would be of most value to the largest number of sentient beings....

Certainly there is an element of mystery in the process of identifying incarnations. But suffice to say that, as a Buddhist, I do not believe that people like Mao or Lincoln or Churchill just "happen."   — *Freedom in Exile*, 215; 218

Sometimes due to misunderstanding the doctrine of karma one has a tendency to blame everything on karma and try to exonerate oneself from responsibility or from the need to take personal initiative. One could quite easily say, "This is due to my negative past karma. What can I do? I am helpless." This is a totally wrong understanding of karma, because although one's experiences are a consequence of one's past deeds, that does not mean that one has no choice, nor that there is no room for initiative to bring about change. — *Healing Anger*, 79

As to the question of how our mental afflictions originate, from the Buddhist point of view one has to accept the Buddha's explanation in terms of the beginningless of consciousness. When talking about the beginninglessness of consciousness, I don't personally think that there is a possibility of coming up with an affirmative argument or reason. Although one can explain it on the basis of tracing the substantial continuum of consciousness, I don't think one can come up with a one hundred percent affirmative proof in the sense of a logical deduction. However, the strongest argument is that if we adopt a contrary position, which is that there is a beginning, then we have to accept that either there is an external creator, an agent, which also leads to problems, or we have to accept some type of uncaused event, one which has no cause and conditions. Again, that is logically incoherent and inconsistent.

So given the choice, the position that the continuum of consciousness is beginningless seems to have fewer logical inconsistencies and contradictions. — *Healing Anger*, 46

Our Scriptures affirm that the moon is a hundred miles above the earth, and that the center of the earth is Mount Meru. If that mountain exists, we should have found it a long time ago, or at least we should have discovered some sign of its existence. Since that isn't the case, we have to distance ourselves from the literal meaning of the Scriptures.

Questioner: And if some refuse to do this?

Dalai Lama: That's their business. It's useless to waste our time arguing with them.   —*Violence and Compassion*, 76

The true gauge by which to evaluate the validity of any [Buddhist] teaching should be whether or not it is true Dharma that serves to liberate us from suffering. If the philosophical views, ethical conduct, and meditative practices of a teacher are in keeping with the teaching of Buddha Shakyamuni and the Indian masters, that is what is most important.

—*Essence of the Heart Sutra*, 72–73

SCIENCE AND SPIRIT

Science and technology cannot replace the age-old spiritual values that have been largely responsible for the true progress of world civilizations as we know it today. No one can deny the material benefits of modern life, but we are still faced with suffering, fear, and tension — perhaps more now than ever before. So it is only sensible to try to strike a balance between material development on the one side and development of spiritual values on the other. In order to bring about a great change, we need to retrieve and strengthen our inner values.

—*How to See Yourself*, 2

Science deals with that aspect of reality and human experience that lends itself to a particular method of inquiry susceptible to empirical observation, quantification and measurement, repeatability, and intersubjective verification — more than one person has to be able to say, "Yes, I saw the same thing. I got the same results." So legitimate scientific study is limited to the physical world, including the human body, astronomical bodies, measurable energy, and how structures work. The empirical findings generated in this way form the basis for further experimentation and for generalizations that can be incorporated into a wider body of scientific knowledge. This is effectively the current paradigm of what constitutes science. Clearly, this paradigm does not and cannot exhaust all aspects of reality, in particular the nature of human existence. In addition to the objective world of matter, which science is masterful at exploring, there exists the subjective world of feelings, emotions, thoughts, and the values and spiritual aspirations based on them. If we treat this realm as though it had no constitutive role in our understanding of reality, we lose the richness of our own existence and our understanding cannot be comprehensive. Reality, including our own existence, is so much more complex than objective scientific materialism allows.

—*The Universe in a Single Atom*, 38–39

The notion of a pre-given, observer-independent reality is untenable. As in the new physics, matter cannot be objectively perceived or described apart from the observer — matter and mind are co-dependent.

This recognition of the fundamentally dependent nature of reality — called "dependent origination" in Buddhism — lies at the very heart of the Buddhist understanding of the world and the nature of our human existence. In brief, the principle of dependent origination can be understood in the following three ways. First, all conditioned things and events in the world come into being only as a result of the interaction of causes and conditions. They don't just arise from nowhere, fully formed. Second, there is mutual dependence between parts and whole; without parts, there can be no whole, without a whole it makes no sense to speak of parts. This interdependence of parts and the whole applies in both spatial and temporal terms. Third, anything that exists and has an identity does so only within the total network of everything that has a possible or potential relation to it. No phenomenon exists with an independent or intrinsic identity. . . .

In physics, the deeply interdependent nature of reality has been brought into sharp focus by the so-called EPR paradox — named after its creators, Albert Einstein, Boris Podolsky, and Nathan Rosen — which was originally formulated to challenge quantum mechanics. Say a pair of particles is created and then separates, moving away from each other in opposite directions — perhaps to greatly distant locations, for example, Dharamsala, where I live, and, say, New York. One of the properties of this pair of particles is that their spin must be in opposite directions — so one is measured "up" and the other will be found to be "down." According to quantum mechanics, the correlation of measurements (for example, when one is up, then the other is down) must exist even though the individual attributes are not determined until the experimenters measure one of the particles, let us say in New York. At that point, the one in New York will acquire a value — let us say up — in which case the other particle must simultaneously become down. These determinations of up and down are instantaneous, even for the particle at Dharamsala, which has not itself been measured. Despite their separation, the two particles appear as an entangled entity. There seems, according to quantum mechanics, to be a startling and profound interconnectedness at the heart of physics.

— The Universe in a Single Atom, 64–65

Once at a public talk in Germany, I drew attention to the growing trend among serious scientists of taking the insights of the world's contemplative traditions into account. I spoke about the meeting ground between my own Buddhist tradition and modern science — especially in the Buddhist arguments for the relativity of time and for rejecting any notion of essentialism. Then I noticed von Weizäcker in the audience, and when I described my debt to him for what little understanding of quantum physics I possess, he graciously commented that if his own teacher Werner Heisenberg had been present, he would have been excited to hear of the clear, resonant parallels between Buddhist philosophy and his scientific insights.

— The Universe in Single Atom, 65

Some more dogmatic Darwinians have suggested that natural selection and survival of the fittest are best understood at the level of individual genes. Here we see the reduction of the strong metaphysical belief in the principle of self-interest to imply that somehow individual genes behave in a selfish way. I do not know how many of today's scientists hold such views. As it stands, the current biological model does not allow for the possibility of real altruism.

At one of the Mind and Life conferences in Dharamsala, the Harvard historian of science Anne Harrington made a memorable presentation on how, and to some extent why, scientific investigation of human behavior has so far failed to develop any systematic understanding of the powerful emotion of compassion. At least in modern psychology, compared with the tremendous amount of attention paid to the negative emotions, such as aggression, anger, and fear, relatively little examination has been paid to more positive emotions, such as compassion and altruism. This emphasis may have arisen because the principal motive in modern psychology has been to understand human pathologies for therapeutic purposes. However, I do feel that it is unacceptable to reject altruism on the ground that selfless acts do not fit with current biological understanding of life

or are simply redefinable as expressions of the self-interest of
the species. This stance is contrary to the very spirit of scientific inquiry. As I understand it, the scientific approach is not
to modify the empirical facts to fit one's theory; rather the
theory must be adapted to fit the results of empirical inquiry.
Otherwise it would be like trying to reshape one's feet to fit
the shoes.

I feel that this inability or unwillingness fully to engage the
question of altruism is perhaps the most important drawback of
Darwinian evolutionary theory, at least in its popular version.
In the natural world, which is purported to be the source of
the theory of evolution, just as we observe competition between
and within species for survival, we observe profound levels of
cooperation (not necessarily in the conscious sense of the term).
Likewise, just as we observe acts of aggression in animals and
humans, we observe acts of altruism and compassion. Why does
modern biology accept only competition to be the fundamental
operating principle and only aggression to be the fundamental trait of living beings? Why does it reject cooperation as an
operating principle, and why does it not see altruism and compassion as possible traits for the development of living beings
as well?   — *The Universe in a Single Atom*, 113–14

POLITICS

I discovered at the age of fifteen the brutal power of politics. I
discovered pitiless imperialism, the cruel desire for conquest, the
so-called law of arms. In my youth communism had a certain
seductive appeal for me. It even seemed to me that a synthe-
sis between Buddhism and communism was possible. Then I
ran up against the incomprehensible contradictions of Chinese
policy — the frenzy of slogans, the intoxication of millions of

brains. I got to know all that in my adolescence and youth. After which came the disappointments, and finally the certainty, that Mao was none other than the "destroyer of Dharma."

— *Violence and Compassion*, 140–41

Not only must the entire social structure undergo a dynamic metamorphosis, but the chief constituent of this structure — the caretaker of society, man — must reevaluate his attitudes, principles and values in order that such a change is seriously effected. Skeptics might question the possibility of altering the social system; but are we not the makers of our environment? Man has created his social dilemmas, and if any change is to happen, the power to make it happen lies with man alone.

— *The Heart of Compassion*, 137

There is a school of thought which warns the moralist to refrain from politics, as politics is devoid of ethics and moral principles. This is a wrong approach, since politics devoid of ethics does not further the benefits to man and his society — and life without morality will make men no better than beasts. The political concept is not axiomatically dirty, a common adjective ascribed to politics today; but the instruments of our political culture have tampered with and distorted the fundamental concepts of fine ideals, to further their own selfish ends.

— *The Heart of Compassion*, 138

I consider it very important for religion to have an influence on politicians. Politicians need religion much more than pious people who have withdrawn from the world need it. There is a constant increase in the scandals in politics and business that can be traced back to the lack of self-discipline on the part of the responsible parties. In India, the minister-president of West Bengal once said to me with what he considered a humble attitude that he was a politician and not a religious person. I responded to him: politicians need religion more than anyone else.

When hermits in solitude are bad persons, the result is that they harm themselves alone and no one else. But when such influential people as politicians are full of bad intentions, they can bring misfortune to many. This is why religion, as continuous work on our inner maturity, is important for political rulers.

—*Path of Wisdom, Path of Peace*, 155–56

Peace is not something which exists independently of us, nor is war. It is true that certain individuals — political leaders, policymakers, army generals — do have particularly grave responsibilities in respect to peace. However, these people do not come from nowhere. They are not born and brought up in outer space. Like us, they were nourished by their mother's milk and affection. They are members of our own human family and have been nurtured within the society which we as individuals have helped create. Peace in the world thus depends on peace in the hearts of individuals. This in turn depends on us all practicing ethics by disciplining our response to negative thoughts and emotions and developing basic spiritual qualities.

—*Ethics for the New Millennium*, 203

If real peace is something more profound than a fragile equilibrium based on mutual hostility, if ultimately it depends on the resolution of internal conflict, what are we to say about war? Although paradoxically the aim of most military campaigns is peace, in reality, war is like fire in the human community, one whose fuel is living people. It also strongly resembles fire in the way it spreads. If, for example, we look at the course of the recent conflict in the former Yugoslavia, we see that what began as a relatively confined dispute grew quickly to engulf the whole region. Similarly, if we look at individual battles, we see that where commanders perceive areas of weakness, they respond by sending in reinforcements — which is exactly like throwing live people onto a bonfire. But because of habituation, we ignore this. We fail to acknowledge that the very nature of war is cold cruelty and suffering.

The unfortunate truth is that we are conditioned to regard warfare as something exciting and even glamorous: the soldiers in smart uniforms (so attractive to children) with their military bands playing alongside them. We see murder as dreadful, but there is no association of war with criminality. On the contrary, it is seen as an opportunity for people to prove their competence and courage. We speak of the heroes it produces, almost as if the greater the number killed, the more heroic the individual. And we talk about this or that weapon as a marvelous piece of technology, forgetting that when it is used it will actually maim and murder living people. Your friend, my friend, our mothers, our fathers, our sisters and brothers, you and me.

What is even worse is the fact that in modern warfare the role of those who instigate it are often far removed from the conflict on the ground. At the same time, its impact on the noncombatants grows even greater. Those who suffer most in today's armed conflicts are the innocent — not only the families of those fighting but, in far greater numbers, civilians who often do not even play a direct role. Even after the war is over, there continues to be an enormous suffering due to land mines and poisoning from the use of chemical weapons — not to mention the hardship it brings. This means that, more and more, women, children, and the elderly are among its prime victims. . . .

Because of the reality of this destructive capacity, we need to admit that, whether they are intended for offensive or for defensive purposes, weapons exist solely to destroy human beings.

But lest we suppose that peace is purely dependent on disarmament, we must also acknowledge that weapons cannot act by themselves. Although designed to kill, so long as they remain in storage, they can do no physical harm. Someone has to push a button to launch a missile strike, or pull a trigger to fire a bullet. No "evil" power can do this. Only humans can. Therefore, genuine world peace requires that we also begin to dismantle the military establishments that we have built. We cannot hope to enjoy peace in its fullest sense while it remains possible for a few individuals to exercise military power and impose their will on others.   —*Ethics for the New Millennium*, 203–6

When, as individuals, we disarm ourselves internally — through countering our negative thoughts and emotions and cultivating positive qualities — we create the conditions for external disarmament. Indeed, genuine, lasting peace will only be possible as a result of each of us making an effort internally. Afflictive emotion is the oxygen of conflict.

—*Ethics for the New Millennium*, 207

The only way to achieve lasting peace is through mutual trust, respect, love, and kindness. The only way. Attempts by global powers to dominate one another through competition in armaments — whether nuclear, chemical, biological, or conventional — is counter productive. How can a world full of hatred and anger achieve real peace? External peace is impossible without inner peace.   —*How to Practice*, 8

HEALTH IN BODY, MIND, WORLD

I think the worst is when people place too much trust or belief in me, in circumstances in which some things are beyond my capability. In such cases, sometimes anxiety, of course, develops. Here, once again, we return to the importance of motivation. Then, I try to remind myself as far as my own motivation is concerned, I am sincere, and I tried my best. With a sincere motivation, one of compassion, even if I made a mistake or failed, there is no cause for regret. For my part, I did my best. Then, you see, if I failed, it was because the situation was beyond my best efforts. So that sincere motivation removes fear and gives you self-confidence. — *Art of Happiness,* 271

Every day I experience the benefits of peace of mind. It's very good for the body. As you might imagine, I am a rather busy man. I take many responsibilities upon myself, activities, trips, and speeches. All that no doubt is a very heavy burden, and still I have the blood pressure of a baby.

Last year in Washington, at the Walter Reed Army Hospital, they took my blood pressure. And the doctor said, "Wow, I wish mine were the same!"

What's good for me is good for other people. I have no doubt on that score. Good food, a struggle against every excessive desire, daily meditation, all that can lead to peace of mind; and peace of mind is good for the body. Despite all the difficulties of life, of which I've had my share, we can all feel that effect.

— *Violence and Compassion,* 75–76

In most cases, the affirmation of the ego leads only to disappointment, or else to conflict with other egos just as exclusive as mine. Especially when the strong development of the ego leads to whims and demands.

The illusion of the permanent self secretes a danger that lies in wait for all of us. I want this, I want that. You might end up killing someone, as we all know well. The excess of egoism leads to uncontrollable perversions, which always end up badly. . . .

But from another standpoint, a firm ego, sure of itself, can be a very positive element. We were talking about the environment, about defending the earth. It's clear that if I decide to carry on that great struggle to save the planet, I have to be sure of myself. Without a very strong sense of self — that is, of its qualities, its possibilities, its conviction — no one can take on such a responsibility. You have to have a real confidence in yourself; that's perfectly clear to me. . . .

If I can return for a moment to the Bodhisattva, who for us is the ideal being, the one who can lay claim to *nirvana*, to absolute repose in the light, but who refuses to attain it, who prefers to remain in contact with this suffering world to come to its aid. In other words, the Bodhisattva will not be able to find his or her rest as long as a trace of suffering subsists in the world. It's not enough to be a regular reader of the sutras! It's not enough to ask where is this or that Bodhisattva? In what direction do I have to prostrate myself? What do I have to say to him?

This Bodhisattva, we have to produce him or her in ourselves. If I tell myself, with conviction, that my task is to put myself at the service of others, for an unspecified period of time, which might not even have an end, that calls for full and complete determination. Without a very strong ego, such determination is impossible.

— *Violence and Compassion*, 118–19

Education is much more than a matter of imparting the knowledge and skills by which narrow goals are achieved. It is also about opening the child's eyes to the needs and rights of others. We must show children that their actions have a universal dimension. And we must somehow find a way to build on their natural

feelings of empathy so that they come to have a sense of responsibility toward others. For it is this which stirs us into action.
Indeed, if we had to choose between learning and virtue, the latter is definitely more valuable. The good heart which is the fruit
of virtue is by itself a great benefit to humanity. Mere knowledge
is not.   —*Ethics for the New Millennium*, 181–82

With regard to the question of the media's emphasis on sex and
violence, there are many factors to consider. In the first instance,
it is clear that much of the viewing public enjoys the sensations
provoked by this sort of material. Secondly, I very much doubt
that those producing material containing a lot of explicit sex
and violence intend harm by it. Their motives are surely just
commercial. As to whether this is positive or negative in itself is
to my mind less important than the question of whether it can
have an ethically wholesome effect. If the result of seeing a film
in which there is a lot of violence is that the viewer's compassion is aroused, then perhaps that depiction of violence would
be justified. But if the accumulation of violent images leads to
indifference, then I think it is not. Indeed, such a hardening of
heart is potentially dangerous. It leads all too easily to lack of
empathy.   —*Ethics for the New Millennium*, 186

The natural world is our home. It is not necessarily sacred or
holy, it is simply where we live. It is therefore in our interest to
look after it. This is common sense. But only recently have the
size of our population and the power of science and technology
grown to the point that they can have a direct impact on nature.
To put it another way, until now, Mother Earth has been able
to tolerate our sloppy house habits. The stage has been reached
where she can no longer accept our behavior in silence. The
problems caused by environmental degradation can be seen as

her response to our irresponsible behavior. She is warning us
that there are limits even to her tolerance.

— *Ethics for the New Millennium*, 188

THE CALL

A revolution is called for, certainly. But not a political, an economic, or even a technical revolution. We have had enough
experience of these during the past century to know that a
purely external approach will not suffice. What I propose is a
spiritual revolution.   — *Ethics for the New Millennium*, 17

My call for a spiritual revolution is thus not a call for a religious revolution. Nor is it a reference to a way of life that is
somehow otherworldly, still less to something magical or mysterious. Rather, it is a call for a radical reorientation away from
our habitual preoccupation with self. It is a call to turn toward
the wider community of beings with whom we are connected,
and for conduct which recognizes others' interests alongside
our own.   — *Ethics for the New Millennium*, 23–24

Love and kindness are the very basis of society. If we lose these
feelings, society will face tremendous difficulties; the survival of
humanity will be endangered. Together with material development, we need spiritual development, so that inner peace and
social harmony can be experienced. Without inner peace, without inner calm, it is difficult to have lasting peace. In this field of
inner development, religion can make important contributions.

— *The Heart of Compassion*, 142

You should realize that whether you achieve Buddhahood or
not, your purpose is to help other sentient beings. Whether you

find yourself in heaven or hell, your purpose is to help other sentient beings. It does not matter how long it takes. You should determine that the altruistic intention to achieve Buddhahood for the sake of all sentient beings will be your only practice, whether you live or die. — *Stages of Meditation,* 76

I have chosen a few lines that I feel would be acceptable to people of all faiths and even to those with no spiritual belief. When reading these lines, if you are a religious practitioner, you can reflect upon the divine form that your worship. A Christian can think of Jesus or God, a Muslim can reflect upon Allah. Then, while reciting these verses, make the commitment to enhance your spiritual values. If you are not religious, you can reflect upon the fact that, fundamentally, all beings are equal to you in their wish for happiness and their desire to overcome suffering. Recognizing this, you make a pledge to develop a good heart. As long as we are part of human society, it is very important to be a kind, warm-hearted person.

> *May the poor find wealth,*
> *Those weak with sorrow find joy.*
> *May the forlorn find new hope,*
> *Constant happiness and prosperity.*
>
> *May the frightened cease to be afraid,*
> *And those bound be free.*
> *May the weak find power,*
> *And may their hearts join in friendship.*
> — *An Open Heart,* 24–25